THE
COMBAT DIARIES

TRUE STORIES FROM THE FRONTLINES OF WORLD WAR II

MIKE GUARDIA

Published by Magnum Books
PO Box 1661
Maple Grove, MN 55311

www.mikeguardia.com

ISBN-13: 979-8-9854285-5-1

For Mom, Dad, Marie and Melanie,
and to the memory of Joan Wipf Nassiri (1954–2022)

Also by Mike Guardia:

American Guerrilla
Shadow Commander
Hal Moore: A Soldier Once…and Always
The Fires of Babylon
Skybreak
Days of Fury
Danger Forward

Co-authored with LTG Harold G. Moore:

Hal Moore on Leadership: Winning When Outgunned and Outmanned

CONTENTS

Acknowledgements   vii

Introduction   ix

Chapter 1- Omaha Red   1

Chapter 2- Dark Violent Seas   10

Chapter 3- Behind Enemy Lines   29

Chapter 4- Dawn Like Thunder   43

Chapter 5- American Spitfire   52

Chapter 6- Eyewitness: Normandy   62

Chapter 7- Battleground: CBI   67

Chapter 8- Frogman   83

Chapter 9- Iwo Jima: In the Shadows of Suribachi   91

Chapter 10- Combat Mailman   101

Chapter 11- One Half Acre of Hell   109

Chapter 12- Ground Zero: Guadalcanal   116

Chapter 13- Commando Kelly   122

Chapter 14- The Longest Winter 136

Chapter 15- GI Jack of All Trades 147

Chapter 16- Blood Alley 161

About the Author 169

ACKNOWLEDGEMENTS

I am indebted to several individuals who helped make this project a reality. First, I give special thanks to Colonel (ret) Don Patton of the *Minnesota World War II Roundtable*—a historical society dedicated to preserving the history of World War II and the oral histories of its veterans. Colonel Patton arranged my meetings with two of the veterans who appear in this volume: Marty Romano and Denzel Alexander. I am also indebted to Dr. Thomas Saylor, PhD; Mr. Al Zdon; and Mr. Ray Merriam, all of whom graciously granted me access to the oral histories and veteran stories they've collected over the years. Special thanks are also reserved for the Pacific War Museum and the Library of Congress. Without the collective help of these individuals and organizations, this book may never have been written.

INTRODUCTION

World War II was the most destructive conflict in human history. At its peak, the US military drew some 16 million men into its ranks to defeat the Axis Powers. They came from nearly every walk of life—farmers, tradesmen, teachers, lawyers, professional athletes, and even Hollywood celebrities. But whether they came from the wheat fields of Kansas, the streets of New York, or the backlots of Tinseltown, these everyday heroes answered the call of duty when their country needed them. They were ordinary men who accomplished extraordinary things. Today, we call them the "Greatest Generation."

The Combat Diaries is a collection of true stories from veterans who served on the frontlines during World War II. Their stories include:

- A young sailor aboard PT-306, who ferried British Commandos and Allied spies onto mainland Europe.
- A young fighter pilot who remains one of the few Americans to fly a British Spitfire into combat.
- A Navy combat diver ("frogman") who swam at night among the Japanese-held islands, defusing underwater mines, and setting demolitions to assist the Marines' amphibious assaults...

...and many more.

Members of the Greatest Generation are leaving us at the rate of several hundred per day. Indeed, the youngest cohort of World War II veterans are now in their nineties. *The Combat Diaries* is a testament to their enduring legacy.

1

OMAHA RED

WILLIAM C. SMITH: THE FIRST MAN ASHORE
ON OMAHA BEACH, RED SECTOR

June 6, 1944. Lieutenant William C. Smith, a young artillery officer and forward observer (FO), steeled himself for the coming invasion. Allied forces were preparing to launch Operation Overlord—a coordinated amphibious/airborne assault into Northern France. "There have been a lot of books written about D-Day," he said.

But Bill had a unique perspective.

"You see, I was the first American on Omaha Red Beach on D-Day…about two hours before the invasion."

On the morning of June 6, there were only two ways for an FO to get to Omaha Beach: (1) Aboard the tactical dinghies, alongside Navy frogmen who would swim ashore hours before the invasion to disarm enemy mines and anti-ship barriers, or (2) aboard the landing craft with the first wave of troops, where they would suffer a 90% casualty rate.

Either way, the odds didn't seem to be in his favor.

In fact, on his first day in the Army, a senior officer told him: "If the Army loses a box of ammunition, there'll be trouble; but second lieutenants are expendable." Moreover, the life expectancy of an FO in the European Theater was less than ten months. "A forward observer's job was simple," Bill said, "just get close enough to the enemy to tell what type of toothpaste they use, and tell the artillery unit exactly where to aim their guns."

A few nights before D-Day, Allied commanders decided to send their forward observers onto the beach with the frogmen, two hours before the invasion. As Bill and his comrades sailed across the English Channel, the admiral in charge told him: "Find yourself a nice spot where you can keep an eye on the Germans."

Easier said than done.

The beaches of Normandy didn't provide much in the way of "hiding spots." Thus, if Bill could see the enemy, then the enemy could likely see him.

"And I would be the only target on the beach, for two hours," he added.

As Bill descended into the rubber raft, the admiral's parting words were clear: "Whatever happens, take good care of that radio. We can replace you, but the radio is important."

It was pitch black during the pre-dawn hours of the Allied invasion—no moon or ambient starlight. "No exterior lights were permitted on the ships for security," said Bill. As he made his way down the rope ladder, he saw that his designated "rubber boat" was more akin to "an oversized truck inner tube with a thin rubber bottom" powered by a cheap electric fan that someone had converted into a motor. Still, this half-baked rubber contrivance was "seaworthy" in the sense that it could float.

Bill settled into the raft alongside three Navy frogmen, detaching from the ship and sailing forward into the moonless night. "I checked to make sure I had my sidearm and extra clips." But then it occurred to him:

"What good is a pistol going to do against all those Germans with all that heavy firepower?"

Still, a Colt .45 was better than nothing. And this wasn't his first invasion, either. Bill had survived the invasions of Sicily and North Africa; and he had already surpassed his 10-month combat life expectancy.

Bill graduated from Ohio State University in 1937 at the tender age of twenty. While still in college, he had started his own insurance business. However, he couldn't *legally* sell insurance until he reached the age of 21. Undeterred, he simply hired a handful of legal-age adults to make his sales until he met the age requirement. A product of Ohio State's Army ROTC program, Bill took a commission in the Army Reserve while devoting his full-time energy to the insurance business. And when Bill was called to active duty in 1940, his father happily ran the agency in his stead. Bill received orders to the 1st Infantry Division on the eve of their initial deployment in 1942. Now, two years later, he was at the cutting edge of what General Eisenhower called the "Great Crusade."

Two days earlier, Bill had seen the invasion fleet in the daylight hours of June 4. "We had been told that 6,000 ships would be involved in the operation, including over 1,200 warships." Now, in the predawn

Lieutenant William C. Smith, US Army.

hours of June 6, he hoped that the invasion fleet was up to the task.

"In studying the aerial photographs," he said, "I had picked out a spot on the rightmost part of our sector." Based on the contours of the terrain, that farthest-right edge seemed to offer the best concealment. "While there were tank traps along most of the beach, this area seemed to be a swimming hole," said Bill. "If any Germans came down to take a dip, my trusty .45 would come in handy. Somehow, with all those

Allied ships in the [English Channel], I doubted if anyone would take the risk."

As the rubber raft churned and sallied towards the beach, its helmsman kept their bearings by way of a small phosphorescent compass. The journey seemed like hours. But when Bill glanced at his watch, he was stunned to see that his rough ride across the English Channel had lasted barely thirty minutes.

Suddenly, their raft turned hard left.

"Ok, the raft is parallel to the wire," whispered the helmsman. "Our bow is pointed in the direction you should find the opening. Good luck."

With that, Bill hoisted his legs over the side, bringing every ounce of his 120-pound frame knee-deep into the frigid waters. He pushed himself away from the raft, wading towards his designated redoubt—the place where, hopefully, he could keep a steady eye on the Germans… and escape detection.

"At that moment, I felt totally alone."

Of course, there were several thousand Germans waiting just beyond the beach.

Wading through the shallows, Bill weaved his way around the obstacles set by the *Wehrmacht*. First were the steel tridents, lined with explosives. "I knew that there would not be anti-personnel mines there because the Germans had to leave room to repair any damage done by the sea." Next came the anti-tank ditch, and its attendant anti-tank wall—a solid concrete barrier that would be troublesome for armored and infantry forces alike. "As I felt hard sand underfoot," he said, "I knew I was out of the water." But he had to get to the softer sand, so he wouldn't get caught in an undertow when the tide came in.

As he looked for his rockbound hiding spot, Bill felt another change in the grainy texture beneath his feet. "It was no longer the sand, but dirt and stone of the service road that ran around the beach. The map I had studied…showed that the road was underwater except at low tide. I crossed the road, and at long last felt the soft sand." He had made it to the beach proper.

After a few more moments of deliberate pace counting and night navigation, Bill found the rock formation that he intended to use for his observation post.

But this rock formation wasn't truly "rock."

The aerial photographs had failed to show that this "rock formation" was actually "an assortment of concrete blocks, piles of junk [and] excess cement." Undaunted, Bill tossed aside enough of the rubble to hide himself up to his shoulders. "I then used the loose rocks to cover all but my eyes, head, and hands." With the radio tucked under his chin, Bill laughed as he realized his newfound observation post made him look like a "turtle in his shell."

As he looked up, Bill could see a few lights from within the German bunkers.

That was odd, he thought to himself.

The Allied naval bombardment was supposed to have knocked out the enemy's power grid.

At daybreak, Bill recalled that the sky was so gray, he could hardly tell where the sea ended and the sky began. Through the gray luster of the morning haze, however, Bill discovered why the enemy's electrical grid was still intact.

The German defenses hadn't been touched.

"The bombing that had taken place before the invasion was supposed to destroy the Germans' ability to fend off the invasion" he said. "Either the bombing had missed the targets…or it had no effect whatsoever. I had the feeling that somewhere in France, there were a lot of dead cows"—victims of misplaced naval gunfire. The Germans, on the other hand, were "dry, well-fed, quite rested, and very well-protected in their concrete hotel." More to the point, these unharmed Germans would soon be directing their own gunfire onto the invasion fleet. "I realized in an instant," he said, "that unless I could call enough fire to silence the guns in those pillboxes, this part of the invasion would not succeed."

At about thirty minutes to H-Hour, Bill saw the first of the Germans' coastal batteries open fire on the Allied fleet. "I located the source of the fire as close as I could." The German battery, likely a group of 88s, fired a volley of ten rounds, all of which landed dangerously close to the destroyer USS *Emmons* and the battleship USS *Arkansas*. Keying his radio, Bill called out to the fleet.

"I registered my first target and gave the order to fire when ready."

The *Arkansas* answered with a volley of its own—twenty rounds of 12-inch naval gunfire, all of which promptly silenced the offending battery.

But when the first Allied shell impacted on the beach, the Germans fired up their searchlights, scanning the shore for anything that looked out of place. The Germans knew that if they were getting such accurate naval gunfire, there must have been an Allied spotter somewhere on the beach. Luckily, the beams of light never found Bill's hiding spot.

The first shot directed against the main German pillbox landed slightly left. "I adjusted [the firing coordinates] and ordered fire at will." A flurry of shells quickly descended into the pillbox, blowing its entire front into a medley of smoke and flames. "It looked like a horizontal volcano," Bill remembered. "That was one less gun the Germans had to kill our men. But there were so many more to hit."

That's when Bill noticed another gun emplacement; this one had been drilled into the side of a nearby cliff. He called for fire, but the incoming rounds fell a bit short. When he called for an adjustment, the shipboard battery liaison replied with:

"We see that target, and we'll get that son of a bitch closed up!"

A moment later, two streams of tracer rounds zoomed overhead, painting the gun emplacement for more follow-on fire. "In the next second," Bill said, "nearly half-a-dozen shells seemed to converge on a single spot"—the exact location of the offending gunfire. "The ground shook under me. A glorious flood of gravel, stone dust, gun parts, and chunks of medium, well-done German gunners fell down like a pouring rain."

But there was no time to celebrate. He had to register fire on the next target.

He soon spied another 88mm gun emplacement, which promptly disappeared under a hail of naval gunfire. "In scanning the area close to the bluff," he recalled, "I didn't see any of our DD tanks [amphibiously-modified Shermans]. I wasn't sure where they were, but I had to keep firing the guns that I had."

German mortar fire began to pepper the beach, but Bill could tell that this was feral, undirected fire. Indeed, the Germans were panicking. By now, they were hoping to land some "lucky punches" through volume of fire. But feral as it was, this incoming mortar fire was enough to disrupt the Allied landings because "our men and equipment occupied such a high percentage of the area."

Nevertheless, Bill kept calling for fire.

It was hard to get accurate counterbattery fire against the mortars because the German mortarmen were *behind* the crest of the bluff. Thus, Bill had to estimate the enemy's position based on the rounds' point of impact. Against these mortars, "I was shooting blind," he said.

As Allied troops began storming the beach, however, Bill realized he now had *two* problems. First, he had to make sure the Allied guns didn't fire on their own men. Second, "I had to be sure that the shots I called would not dump tons of concrete on our men" as they got to the bottom of the cliff.

After calling fire on another 88, Bill turned his attention towards a pillbox on a nearby cliff. He was ready to rain fire on the pillbox, but stopped himself as he saw a squad of Americans climbing ropes towards the top of that same cliff.

These climbing soldiers quickly neutralized the target.

"Another emplacement was just over the top of the bluff," he continued. "By this time our troops had reached the area but were unable to take the pillbox because of the firing coming out of it." Bill called for fire on the offending pillbox, but the naval shells hit just below the target. "I moved the shot up," he said, "but the second shell hit in almost the exact same spot." Luckily, a nearby destroyer, taking stock of the same enemy pillbox, opened fire with a volley of shells from its forward battery, obliterating the entire front end of the bluff. "That captain risked his men in support of our invasion," Bill recalled.

By this point, Bill was running on pure adrenaline. He had no idea how long he'd been on the beach, but he dared not look at his watch. In fact, he had taped over the watch's luminescent dial, lest it draw attention from a sharp-eyed enemy. All he knew was that he had been awake for the past 48 hours, and he was getting exhausted.

But this was no time to rest.

"I had to keep finding targets and destroying them."

That's when Bill noticed the German self-propelled guns firing from the edge of the bluff. "They would fire, then move back out of sight." Bill registered more gunfire in their direction; and although he knocked out a few of the mobile guns, he couldn't get *all* of them. Still, he kept calling for fire even after his voice had gone hoarse. "Again and again, the shots pummeled the fortresses on the shore," he said. "The enemy fire slowly but clearly dwindled down as the fire from the ships and our men on the beach took a toll on their defenses."

As the battle began to wane, a group of Army Rangers scaled to the top of the bluff and "captured the few remaining enemy still fighting."

After that, the enemy fire stopped.

"The only noises at that point were coming from the reinforcements and equipment coming on shore." Bill finally removed the tape from his watch, and glanced at the time.

"It was almost noon," he said.

He had been on the beach for eight hours.

He then had his first sustained look at the carnage along the shore. "It was indescribably horrible," he said. "There were thousands of bodies on the beach and in the water. I was sick to my stomach. I had done everything I could, but I still wasn't able to prevent the terrible slaughter of so many brave men." Closing his eyes, Bill let out a muffled prayer:

"God, please take care of these brave men that gave their lives to free this land. They deserve your personal attention. Amen."

Bill survived the incursion at Omaha Red, and he participated in many of the 1st Infantry Division's signature campaigns across Europe. In the years and decades following the war, however, Bill often sparred with a number of armchair historians and rear echelon commentators who doubted his claims of being the first man on Omaha Red. "After I gave a speech to a multi-service support committee in 2002," he said, "a [retired] general...came up and began to argue with me about how I got to the beach." The indignant general said: "I have seen the official records. You had to have gone in with the first wave of men and were not possibly on the beach before the invasion."

Bill was not impressed.

"General, what war were you in?"

"Korea."

"I thought so," said Bill. "You look far too young to have been in World War II. Besides I don't remember seeing you or any other high-ranking official at H-Hour -2."

"Well, no but..."

Realizing that Bill had just destroyed his argument, the general tried a different approach.

"I wanted to ask about the ships that you claim were used to fire on the German defenses. I can't see how a couple of 6 or 8-inch shells would destroy a cement pillbox so completely." Bill interjected: "As I said, the battleship USS *Arkansas* was there and used its 12-inch guns to hit the box." Bill punctuated the remark by saying there were several dead Germans who would disagree with the general's assessment.

And by now, the general's resilience was fading fast.

"I...wasn't sure," he stammered, "not sure...even 12-inch guns could do that much damage."

"General," said Bill, "I'm sure that the 88 in the pillbox had several shells standing by for rapid fire when it was hit by the multiple 12-inch shells. The entire box became concrete snowflakes drifting down like Christmas in June."

By now, the general knew he had been bested...and respectfully withdrew.

After the war, Bill remained in the Army Reserve for a number of years, and later became president of the Reserve Officers Association. Returning home to Ohio, he sold his insurance agency and joined the ER Kissinger Company—his father-in-law's photo finishing business. He eventually became the company's general manager, and expanded its operations to encompass 82% of the photo finishing market in central Ohio. He later formed the inaugural Sales Marketing Department at Columbus Technical Institute, which became one of the most-respected marketing operations in the Midwest.

Even in retirement, Bill refused to stay idle. He became an active member in the VFW and participated in several events commemorating World War II and the Normandy landings.

He passed away on July 15, 2011 at the age of 93.

2

DARK VIOLENT SEAS

Marty Romano & *PT-306*

The story of Marty Romano begins in the concrete jungles of Jersey City. Born on June 11, 1924, he was the fifth of seven children born to Gasparé and Margarita Romano—both of whom were Italian immigrants. As was typical in many Italian families, said Marty, "my mother was very hard and domineering; the matriarch of our family." Together, his parents ran a dry goods store in Jersey City—an established business serving the city's ever-growing population of Irish and Italian immigrants. And, as with many family-owned businesses, young Marty was expected to help run the store when he wasn't in school. "I would carry all the linens and the draperies," he said with a chuckle.

Marty's childhood was typical of most boys who grew up in the working-class neighborhoods of New Jersey. He enjoyed playing football and baseball, but the shortage of greenspace in Jersey City meant that he often found himself playing street hockey or stickball. During the summers, and after school, he and his brother would earn extra money by working on cars. "My brother and I polished cars and repaired dented fenders," he said. "I never worked in a garage, but I was able to take some cars apart. In fact, when I was dating my wife, Lorraine, I got up early one morning, took my Buick apart, and had it back together in time for my date that evening!" Aside from detailing the normal variety of Fords and Chevrolets, Marty remembered the fanciest cars he worked on were Packards. Indeed, Packards were considered the premiere luxury cars in America prior to World War II.

In many ways, Marty Romano was also a product of his time. His was the generation raised on the harrowing tales of the Great War, the decadence of the Roaring Twenties, and the economic hardships of the Great Depression. Although money was tight (as it was for most families during that era), the Romanos' dry goods store, and the five-unit apartment building they owned, kept the family solvent.

It was, however, a time when many Italian-Americans were either discriminated against, or looked upon with suspicion. To make matters worse, Italy itself had fallen into the orbit of fascism. Under the brutal reign of Benito Mussolini, Italy aligned itself with Nazi Germany, becoming a full partner in the newly-formed Axis Powers. Still, many Americans hoped that the saber-rattling of fascist dictators would run its course without their involvement.

But by the time Marty began his freshman year at Dickinson High School in 1937, the political climate in Europe was devolving further into chaos. Within the next two years, Adolf Hitler would annex Austria, invade Czechoslovakia, and make a public fool of British Prime Minister Neville Chamberlain, promising "peace" in exchange for territorial concessions. These illusions of peace were quickly shattered, however, on September 1, 1939 when Germany invaded Poland—the opening rounds of a yearlong blitzkrieg that would bury half of Europe.

But as Europe plunged itself into another war, Marty Romano busied himself with the normal variety of high school activities. Since his mother had forbidden him to play on the school's sports teams, he joined whatever school clubs were available. "My mother took my hockey stick and she had my father chop up my skates! So, any sport I played was hidden from her. She was stern but very protective." Marty remembers that when his father chopped the skates at Mom's insistence, he gave his son a look of resignation.

"Look, I have to live with her," he told Marty. "So, I gotta get rid of these skates."

These semi-idyllic routines were interrupted, however, on the afternoon of December 7, 1941. Marty was in the kitchen, having just returned from Sunday Mass, when the radio announcer broke in with the bulletin that Pearl Harbor had been bombed. Like most other Americans, Marty was stunned.

"What the hell does this mean?" he asked. "What are we going to do now?"

No one had expected a first strike against Hawaii, much less from the Japanese. To this point, nearly everyone had considered Japan's military to be an inferior force. Conventional wisdom said that the threat would come from Nazi Germany long before it came from the Japanese. The following day, the US declared war on the Empire of Japan.

The Crew of *PT-306*. Marty Romano is in the front row, second from right (kneeling).

Germany soon responded, however, by declaring war on the United States, thus forcing the US into a two-front conflict. Although Japan had initiated hostilities, the US adopted a "Europe First" policy—meaning that, while fighting on two fronts, Europe would be the priority. The reasoning behind this decision was that Germany could win the war without Japan, but Japan couldn't win the war without Germany.

Marty Romano, meanwhile, had graduated from Dickinson High School in 1941 and spent the next two years working as a machinist's apprentice, tooling subcomponents for firearms—skills that would serve him well when he joined the Navy in 1943. As a civilian machinist, he learned first-hand the excruciating precision that goes into manufacturing quality products. "I learned how to work within *1/10,000th* of an inch!" he exclaimed. Indeed, every subcomponent of the gun had to be measured within a specific tolerance, or the weapon wouldn't fire.

In the summer of 1943, Marty reported to the local induction center at the Newark Armory. Like many of his contemporaries, he had been drafted, but his work as a machinist had made him a prime candidate for the Navy. It was the branch of service that had an entire career field dedicated to his trade—the ubiquitous "Machinist's Mate" (MM). They would be trained as shipboard engineers, maintaining and troubleshooting the propulsion and auxiliary systems. Most of their time would be spent below deck, but their job was just as critical to maintaining the ship's warfighting functions. For without a steady crew of engineers, a ship would be literally "dead in the water."

Naturally, Mama Romano was none too thrilled that her son—the boy whom she had tried to shield from the perils of team sports—was going off to war. "I know she felt lousy that I had to go," he said. But Marty was proud to do his patriotic duty. On September 24, 1943, he was sworn into the United States Navy and reported to boot camp in Newport, Rhode Island.

All at once, Marty's new name was "Boot,"—the moniker given to all new sailors when they arrived for recruit training. After getting his inoculations and a standard-issue buzz haircut, he packed up his civilian attire, trading it for the normal variety of Naval uniforms. With little regard to size, or even proper fit, the Navy doled out these uniforms with the expectation that sailors would wear them to standard. The next issued item was his sleeping gear. In true naval fashion, they issued him a hammock with mattress, two mattress covers, two blankets, and a pillow. To store this ever-growing list of issued items, Marty and his new shipmates were each given a "Sea Bag"—the ubiquitous three-foot-long canvas duffle bag. As with everything else he received, Marty stenciled his name onto the side of the bag. His final gift that day was a copy of *The Bluejackets' Manual*—the so-called "Sailor's Bible." Its pages contained everything Marty needed to know about becoming a sailor.

Admittedly, boot camp was a culture shock. "I was out of shape," he said, "but they got me into shape in short order!" Indeed, every morning the drill instructors would take the recruits on endurance runs—steadily increasing the distance traveled every week. Aside from the exhaustive physical training, Marty also had to learn the basics of shipboard operations and damage control. Any ship could be a fickle mistress—and even the most innocuous things could throw her off balance, or cripple her ability to fight.

It was also during boot camp that Marty had his first exposure to the Patrol Torpedo boats. These "PT boats," as they were called, had become somewhat of a novelty within the Allied naval forces. By design, they were small and agile, relying on stealth and speed to launch torpedoes at enemy warships. PT boats typically had crews of 12-14 men, and carried four torpedoes as its primary armament. Marty first noticed the Patrol Torpedo boats during boot camp as they went sailing by, en route to the PT Center in nearby Melville, Rhode Island.

At first, Marty didn't know what to make of these newfangled PT boats.

"They're not big enough to be destroyers," he told himself.

Yet, they were too big to be gunboats.

But, whatever their classification, these boats carried guns, torpedoes, *and* they could engage the enemy at close range.

"So, yeah, I was impressed."

Upon completing boot camp, he volunteered for PT duty and arrived at Melville the following week from Newport.

As a newly-minted sailor and machinist's mate, Marty received the proverbial "crash course" on how to maintain the PT boat's massive engine suite: the triple-tandem Packard 3M-2500. Indeed, the same luxury automobile company whose cars Marty had polished in Jersey City was now manufacturing combat engines. Like other automotive giants of the day, Packard had converted its facilities to wartime production. Aside from producing PT boat engines, Packard also developed the V-1650, which powered the P-51 Mustang fighter.

The Packard engine would become Marty's "bread and butter" for the duration of the war. It was a twelve-cylinder, liquid-cooled powertrain capable of speeds in excess of 45 knots. Like most naval engines, however, the Packard 2500 series was a "gas hog." In fact, even at a cruising speed of 32 knots, the Packard consumed more than 200 gallons of fuel per hour. As such, the standard PT boat had to carry some 3,000 gallons of reserve fuel, just enough for the crew to make a 12-hour patrol.

"We also had to learn the silhouettes of the Japanese and German warships," he recalled. PT boats were expected to fight at night, and memorizing silhouettes was the surest way to guarantee that a sailor could recognize an enemy ship during low visibility. "We also had to recognize enemy aircraft," particularly the enemy's naval aviation assets. Although the PT boat wasn't optimized for anti-aircraft fire, its secondary .50 caliber machine guns could easily elevate and traverse to engage low-flying aircraft.

In the spring of 1944, Marty graduated from the PT Training Center and boarded the USS *Ranger* (the famed aircraft carrier) en route to Casablanca. That fabled city in North Africa had become one of the primary hubs for incoming Allied personnel. "By that time," he said, "the North African campaign was completed, Sicily was captured, Salerno was in Allied hands, and Anzio was in the mopping-up phase. That's when and where I came into this theater."

But although the Allies had gained control of North Africa (and most of Italy), the *Kriegsmarine* and *Regia Marina* were still running patrols throughout the Mediterranean. "When I got to North Africa, they horded us off the ship and into these 'Forty-and-Eight' railroad cars." These "Forty-and-Eights" were a common sight throughout Europe and North Africa. It was little more than a standard boxcar; and its name was a direct reference to its rated stowage capacity: forty men or eight horses. During both World Wars, the Allies had adapted the Forty-and-Eight as a troop transport. As expected, however, these troop-carrying boxcars lacked even the most basic amenities found aboard the standard passenger trains. Marty recalled that they were cramped, unsanitary, and poorly-ventilated.

"Cattle were treated better!" he laughed.

Throughout the first leg of the trip (on approach to Algiers), Marty enjoyed the occasional respite of climbing atop the boxcar for some fresh air. Indeed, a rooftop view of the North African landscape was better than sitting among the sweltering heat of 60-70 sailors packed into a 40-capacity railcar. Marty would have stayed atop the Forty-and-Eight for the remainder of the trip...had it not been for the swarm of locusts that greeted him outside of Algiers.

"There were thousands of them! And I don't know where they came from."

Perhaps the rail line went through their nesting ground, and the swarm had been vexed by the sudden appearance (and attendant noise) of a steam locomotive. But Marty, not wanting to endure another Old Testament plague, reluctantly settled back into the railcar.

"We were on that miserable cattle car for days," he said, "through Algiers, Oren, and Tunis." For food, Marty and his friends had nothing more than the standard "C" and "K" Rations. Because there were no bathrooms aboard the train, Marty recalled that: "We made a deal with the engineer." One blast of his whistle would indicate that a heavily-vegetated area was coming up; this would offer some degree of privacy for the sailors who had to relieve themselves. Two whistle blasts indicated that it was time to get back on board.

Arriving at the Replacement Depot in Tunis, Marty discovered that he'd been assigned to Motor Torpedo Squadron 15 (RON 15). At the time, RON 15 was stationed on La Maddalena, an island nestled among the narrow straits between Corsica and Sardinia. It was now May 1944, and the tide was turning in the Allies' favor. Over the past year, American forces had tightened their grip on the Mediterranean, and were slowly rolling back the tide of Japanese aggression in the Pacific. Meanwhile, these young torpedo boat squadrons were proving their mettle in both theaters of the war. In fact, the Japanese had begun calling them "devil boats" and the "mosquito fleet"—begrudgingly admiring the boldness and tenacity of American PT crews.

As it turned out, Marty's assignment to RON 15 was short-lived. In fact, he had barely set foot on La Maddalena when he was transferred to Motor Torpedo Squadron 22 (RON 22) in Bastia, Corsica.

"They needed a replacement engineman," he said. "I was it."

The new assignment put him aboard *PT-306*, nicknamed "The Fascinatin' Bitch." There were no pretenses of political correctness back then…and a ship's crew could choose any colorful nickname they wanted.

"Around this time, we invaded Elba, an island off the northwest coast of Italy. Both squadrons—RON 15 and RON 22—were involved in this operation." The invasion was carried out by the Free French Forces, supported by US and Royal Navy assets. "Before the invasion," Marty recalled, "I happened to be in the town square of Bastia, Corsica, and there was General De Gaulle—a tall, gaunt man rallying the crowd." Since the Fall of France in 1940, Charles De Gaulle had become the leader of the Free French Forces, an amalgamated resistance to the Vichy government run by Marshal Petain.

As May turned to June, Marty Romano completed the first of his 63 combat missions aboard *PT-306*. June 1944 was a watershed moment for the Allied cause. Operation Overlord (the invasion of Normandy), marked the beginning of the end for the Third Reich. However, the *Wehrmacht* still had a foothold on the Italian Peninsula, and they were prepared to defend every last inch of it. Reflecting on his first mission, Marty said: "I have to admit that an eerie feeling came over me when I saw the Italian coast for the first time. This was the land of my forefathers."

For the PT crews, their orders were simple: find, interdict, and destroy any Axis warships operating near the Italian coast or the Tuscan

Archipelago. However, they also had the curious mission of ferrying Allied spies to and from the Italian mainland. In fact, during his first few months aboard *PT-306*, it seemed that Marty and his shipmates were little more than a taxi service for the OSS and their Allied variety of field agents. These spies and saboteurs would often be dropped behind enemy lines, gathering intelligence on Axis troop movements before being picked up on the nighttime shore by a designated PT boat.

On any given day, Marty and his shipmates knew little of what was happening in the broader context of the war. Aside from the occasional news briefing, radio broadcast, or letter from home, the men of *PT-306* had limited information about the trajectory of the Allied campaign. During his night missions along the coast, however, Marty recalled seeing the muzzle flashes of the dueling tank and artillery positions along the mainland. The southern flashes, of course, were coming from the Allied ground troops. The northern gunfire, however, belonged to the fledgling German troops and the Mussolini loyalists. Yet, every night, Marty noticed that these dueling muzzle flashes were slowly migrating northward—indicating that the Allies were gaining ground against the enemy.

As an engineer, Marty split his time between the engine room and manning the guns on deck during his rotational watch duties. Indeed, every member of the PT crew had to be proficient in the use of defensive armaments, even if he wasn't a gunner's mate. Below deck, Marty and three other engineers kept a close eye on the Packard powertrains. "We would service the boat early in the afternoon," he said, "checking gas, oil, and getting her ready for mission." While underway, however, the engines were so loud that Marty and his fellow engineers had to communicate through written messages or lip-reading.

At a cruising speed of 32 knots, the engines were relatively easy to maintain. But even at lower speeds, the triple-tandem Packard engines were not immune to breakdowns or operational hiccups. For example, Marty recalled one mission where the skipper ordered "full reverse." Said Marty: "The engines were shifted out of the forward gear, right into reverse, but this sudden maneuver froze the engines! And there we were, dead in the water."

Soon, their sister PT boats (part of a three-ship formation) began pulling away, unaware that *306* was now immobilized.

"We then sprang into action."

Remembering that automobiles could be "push-started" (i.e., pushing the car fast enough and popping the clutch), they attempted a similar maneuver with the onboard Packard engines. "We got one engine running," he said, "and we had the Skipper rev the engine to maximum RPM." As *PT-306* lurched forward into the waves, "the second engine went off," said Marty, "so now we had two engines going, and we did the same thing with the third."

Temperamental engines aside, Marty's most memorable moment aboard *PT-306* was a near-brush with fratricide. "We took care of the night patrols, and during the daylight hours our aircraft would take over." One day at dawn, while coming back from a nighttime mission near Genoa, the skipper of *PT-306*, Lieutenant John Groweg, said:

"Well, let's make one more pass."

Likely, Groweg wanted to use the morning daylight to get a clearer look at the Italian coastline. But as *PT-306* ambled off the Genoese coast, Marty spied a plane overhead.

"Say, Skipper, take a look."

Groweg could tell by its markings that the plane was American.

"He's one of us," Groweg assured him. "He's all right."

But this American pilot had just identified *PT-306* as an enemy ship.

The *Kriegsmarine* and *Regia Marina* operated their own fleets of motor torpedo boats—respectively termed "E-boats" and "MAS boats." And, to a fatigued or untrained eye, these Axis torpedo craft could closely resemble an American PT boat.

"Sure enough," said Marty, "he opened fire, and I could see tracers coming straight out of the plane's wings."

Luckily, no one was killed by the friendly fire. But the strafing did cause considerable damage to another PT boat running the same mission alongside *306*. Sadly, that misplaced fire killed one sailor aboard the second PT.

"Hold your fire!" Groweg yelled. "He's one of us."

The pilot came around for another pass, but aborted the mission as soon as he realized the boats were American. "Somehow, he got the word," said Marty—but the crewmen of *PT-306* were alert and ready for action.

"How had the pilot mistaken us for an enemy ship?" Marty wondered.

"We had our radar on...our bow was painted. We were flying American pennants and the stern was painted the colors we were supposed to have." Yet, even with seemingly-ideal control measures, this incident demonstrated that no ship was immune to the ever-lurking danger of fratricide.

Shortly after the invasion of Elba, *PT-306* had a chance encounter with one of its Italian counterparts: *MAS 562*. On the night of June 29, 1944, while patrolling the northern coast of Elba, *PT-308* and *PT-309* encountered two MAS torpedo boats trying to infiltrate the harbor at Portoferraio. Both PTs opened fire at 800 yards, prompting the enemy vessels to run north, returning fire with their 20mm guns. *PT-308* and *309* gave chase for nearly ten miles until *MAS 562* began to fall back. As they closed in on the fledgling enemy boat, the PT crews noticed that *MAS 562* had caught fire. The Italian crew, in their panic, had jumped overboard, leaving *MAS 562* to its fate. The PT boats, meanwhile, recovered some fourteen surviving sailors from *MAS 562*, including the commander of the Italian MAS fleet at La Spezia. All fourteen sailors were ferried back to Corsica where they were turned over to the Master-at-Arms for prisoner processing and debriefing.

Following that mission, *PT-308* and *309* had reported *MAS 562* destroyed and sunk. Considering that the ship was badly burning when the PTs left the scene, it was logical to assume that *MAS 562* had succumbed to its wounds. The following morning, however, the Army Air Forces liaison officer approached RON 22, saying: "Hey, you guys put in a claim for this boat. It's still alive; and it's still out at sea." Indeed, aerial reconnaissance had confirmed that *MAS 562* was still burning off the coast of Elba, and it hadn't sunk.

Thus, RON 22 dispatched *PT-306* to recover the Italian torpedo boat, put out the fire, and tow it back to Elba. By the time *PT-306* arrived at the floating wreckage, however, "it had been stripped," Marty laughed. "You better believe it had been stripped!" Indeed, another MAS or PT crew had stripped *562* of most of its valuable hardware. Marty did, however, manage to secure two token souvenirs from *MAS 562*—a small mandolin and a brass warning placard for the ship's alarm system that read: "It is forbidden to use the alarm signal without plausible reason."

Still, Marty was fascinated by how the American PT boats differed from their MAS counterparts. For example, the Italian torpedo boats had two engines, whereas the American PTs had three. "The Italian boat had an auxiliary engine on the same shaft," Marty recalled. In fact, the layout and mechanical bearings of the MAS powerplant reminded him of the latter-day Ford Model T engines.

None of the PT crews ever learned why the MAS boats had been lingering off the shores of Portoferraio that night. However, it was possible that the Italian crews had gone there to evacuate the "high-

PT-306. Marty Romano is seated at the helm.

ranking German officers who had evaded capture by the occupying forces."

While wrangling enemy ships and patrolling the Italian coast, Marty and his shipmates also became adept at dodging enemy sea mines. "That was a crude thing the Germans and Italians would do," he said. "They knew where we were operating and, all of a sudden, we'd see these mines bobbing up and down in our path." Because they were highly visible, Marty shot many of these naval mines from a distance, using the onboard machine guns. He was hoping to see a forced detonation, but these mines would only detonate if they were hit in precisely the right place. Thus, Marty watched in disappointment as his bullet holes simply riddled the floating mines, allowing the sea water to trickle in, and sink from the resulting loss of buoyancy.

By August 1944, the Allies were preparing for Operation Dragoon— the invasion of Southern France. It had been nearly two months since the D-Day landings in Normandy, and the Allies were making steady progress across the battlefields of Northern France. "The invasion of Southern France and Northern France were scheduled [originally] for the same day, June 6," said Marty. "What happened was that there were just not enough ships to invade both the North and the South at the same time. So, Northern France got the priority...and that took most of the ships."

Before the invasion of Southern France, *PT-306* moved to Calvi, on the northwestern side of Corsica. *PT-306* had been assigned to ferry a unit of British Commandos to the beaches between St. Tropez and Cannes. "We were trained to put them in these rubber boats," he said—tactical rubber dinghies that would allow the Commandos to wade ashore undetected by the Axis defenders. After releasing the Commandos into their rubber rafts, *PT-306* would then take up its patrol station in the Ligurian Sea, ready to counter any enemy ships in the area.

With D-Day in Southern France set for August 15, 1944, *PT-306* departed Corsica late on the afternoon of the 14th. "We caught up with the invasion fleet between Corsica and Italy," he said. "And at 1:40 in the morning on August 15, we were at our landing site between St. Tropez and Cannes. Thankfully, the minesweepers had cleared a path… and we went in. We discharged 69 Commandos into those rubber boats. Meanwhile, four other PTs teamed up with three British gunboats and headed towards Genoa, simulating a big task force." This diversionary landing was orchestrated, in large part, by Lieutenant Commander Douglas Fairbanks—the Hollywood actor who joined the Navy and organized the famous "Beach Jumper" program (one of the Navy's first special warfare units).

Not talking above a whisper, Marty and his shipmates helped the Commandos into their rubber dinghies. As the Commandos floated away, Lieutenant Groweg steered *PT-306* back towards the Ligurian Sea. Unfortunately, none of the British Commandos made it to their inland destination. "I found out later that one of the Commandos tripped a land mine and alerted the Germans who opened fire, killing a few. Some returned to the drop-off point looking for us. Unfortunately, we were gone. The rest were taken prisoner."

For the next three days, *PT-306*, along with two other boats from RON 22, were assigned to guard an Allied communications ship anchored off the coast of San Remo. "There were a lot of generals and admirals aboard that ship," Marty recalled. "We had Admirals King and Davidson; General Divers, Wilson, Patch, and others." *PT-306*'s mission was to circle the ship on a 24-hour roving patrol and escort its personnel from ship to shore. "On one such trip," said Marty, "I recall coming up out of the engine room and I notice a guy dressed in khakis with a [Colt] .45 stuck in his hip pocket, one foot on a depth charger, reading a communique."

Curious, Marty asked one of his shipmates: "Who's he?"

"He's your boss," the shipmate replied. "That's Secretary of the Navy Forrestal."

James Forrestal would later become the inaugural Secretary of Defense in 1947.

On the second day of their guard mission, while tethered to the communications ship, the crew of *PT-306* was enjoying an afternoon lull in their daily operations. "Some of us were on deck," Marty recalled, "while others were below - relaxing, sleeping, playing cards, or writing letters when we heard an alarm aboard the ship and the call to General Quarters."

Trouble was on its way.

"Within seconds., I quickly jumped down into the engine room, started the engines, and reported to my battle station." As it turned out, a German reconnaissance plane had been detected several miles out, and the PT boats were taking defensive action. The Navy couldn't afford to lose a communications ship, especially one that carried so many flag officers. "We separated from the ship and laid down a smokescreen. By obscuring visibility from the air, the PT crews hoped to thwart the incoming recon mission. "By the time that reconnaissance plane showed up," said Marty, "the ship was engulfed in smoke"—completely invisible to the prying eyes of the *Luftwaffe*.

As their guard mission ended, *PT-306* was tasked to follow some Navy rowboat commandos into the harbor of Nice, France. *PT-306*'s mission was to pick up maps for the heavy cruisers and battleships to coordinate their inland strikes. But *PT-306* had to follow the rowboat pilots into the harbor because they knew where the enemy sea mines had been laid. "You could see the mines as we passed."

"Events started to slow down for us after that operation," Marty recalled. Finding themselves with little to do, the crew of *PT-306* enjoyed the rare treat of sustained leisure time. Indeed, from the decks of their PT boat, Marty and his shipmates would dive into the Mediterranean for a leisurely swim. "We'd go swimming while the cruisers and battleships were lobbing shells overhead." As Allied ground forces moved farther inland, the naval task force continued pounding away at Axis positions in Italy and Southern France. All told, the naval gunfire was an interesting soundtrack to accompany the PT crew's swimming soiree.

"In September, we went back to Tunis, Africa for new engines, repairs, and mandatory shots for the bubonic plague,"—still a lingering health hazard in that part of the world. RON 22 then settled into its new base in Antibes, France. As the Allied ground forces moved farther up the European mainland, the naval bases moved accordingly. "We operated out of this base for the next two months, and then in November, we moved to Livorno, Italy. November and December were heavy duty. We went out on missions every night, foul or fair."

By this point in the war, however, German and Italian naval activity had fallen to near-negligible levels. As such, most of the latter-day patrols for *PT-306* passed without incident. But the hours of boredom were frequently punctuated by moments of heart-pounding terror. On one occasion, *PT-306* happened upon a French cruiser, southbound off the coast of Monte Carlo.

"We didn't know where the hell it was coming from," he said.

"And why was it coming through *here*?"

In the low visibility, Marty couldn't tell if the ship was friendly or enemy. But, manning his .50 caliber machine gun, he was ready to open fire if the ship failed to identify itself. *PT-306* challenged the cruiser, whereupon the French vessel rendered the appropriate "friendly" signal, indicating that she was an Allied ship.

The crewmen of *PT-306* breathed a heavy sigh of relief.

"That was pretty scary," Marty admitted. "The adrenaline was going."

Moreover, "I had a puny .50 caliber machine gun, compared to the 3-to 5-inch guns looking down at us!" Tacitly, Marty admitted that if the cruiser had been enemy, there was *nothing* his .50 cal could have done to stop the bigger ship or its gun batteries.

Marty also had several encounters with Italian dynamite boats. "What the Italians would do," he said, "was get a speed boat, load it up with dynamite, then try to ram us and blow us up." In their desperation, these die-hard Mussolini loyalists had created their own version of a *kamikaze* attack. The Italians' success rate, however, was far below that of their Japanese brethren. One night, while on watch, Marty spotted a silhouette that was typical of the Italian suicide boats.

"I see it! I see it!" he yelled to the skipper.

"Where?" asked the skipper.

Marty pointed to a spot on the horizon, where the breaking waves gave the telltale sign of an attack craft on approach. Calling the crew to General Quarters, Lieutenant Groweg gave them simple instructions:

"Where Marty's firing, you follow!"

Manning the twin .50 caliber guns, Marty Romano initiated the opening fusillade, his tracer rounds "painting" the target for his shipmates as they joined into the melee. Soon, every crew-served weapon aboard

PT-306 was firing in unison at the oncoming suicide boat.

Their efforts were not in vain.

For within less than 100 yards, the Italian suicide boat sank beneath the waves.

That December, Marty earned his eligibility for replacement, and was given a 33-day furlough back to the United States. During World War II, a PT sailor's eligibility for furlough was based on the number of missions he had served. After a certain number of missions, the Navy realized that a sailor would begin to suffer from "operational fatigue," thus losing their edge in the game of naval combat. After completing 63 missions, Marty Romano was tapped for rotation, along with two other shipmates from *PT-306*. "We were going back to Sardinia to pick up our replacements, and there they were." As *PT-306* underwent more repairs and maintenance, Marty handed off the engine room duties to his replacement. With orders authorizing his 33-day furlough back to the United States, Machinist's Mate 3d Class Marty Romano departed RON 22 on December 27, 1944.

By December 1944, the Allied offensive in Europe had stalled under the Germans' counterattack in the Ardennes Forest of France. History would call it the Battle of the Bulge. Soon, however, the Allied offensive was back on track; and by February 1945, the Allies had penetrated deep into the Fatherland.

Marty Romano, meanwhile, boarded a Navy supply ship back to the US. "There were three of us in the squadron that all went home together," he recalled—all of whom coincidentally lived in the greater New York City area. Landing at Norfolk on February 6, 1945, Marty and two fellow sailors, Gab Costello and Tony Sica, travelled up the East Coast to see their families. Marty recalled that seeing his mother, father, and siblings was the best homecoming present he could have wanted. As part of the celebration, his father opened a 50-gallon keg of homemade wine.

As it turned out, Marty's elder brother, Joseph, was serving in the Marshall Islands. And Mom Romano, now with multiple sons in the war, was elated to have young Marty back home, even if only for 33 days. After all, the country was still at war, and many sailors were being redeployed to the Pacific. Thus, it came as little surprise when, at the conclusion of his 33-day leave, Marty received orders to the Pacific theater.

It was now March 1945. Following the renewed Allied offensive on mainland Europe, it was clear that Nazi Germany was in its last throes. Meanwhile, in the Pacific, the enemy strongholds on Tarawa, Saipan, and Iwo Jima had collapsed under the fury of the "island hopping" campaign. That summer, the Japanese would fight their last losing battle on the island of Okinawa.

But for Marty Romano, the more pressing matter was simply *getting* to the Pacific theater. He had been ordered to report to PT Base 17 in the Philippines, whereupon he'd be assigned to any PT boat that needed a replacement. Departing from San Francisco aboard a troop carrier, he found the voyage to be an unusual affair. Onboard were several members of the WAVES (the US Navy Women's Reserve), all of whom were tightly-guarded by Marine Corps MPs. It was a slightly comical, albeit necessary, control measure: The skipper didn't want any romantic liaisons en route to the Philippines.

Mid-voyage, however, the captain suddenly vectored his ship onto a new course, deliberately sailing to cross the 180th Meridian (International Date Line) and the Equator at their point of intersection. According to naval traditions, such a maneuver would induct the ship's crew into an elite company of seafarers.

"Now, I did *not* think this was a good idea!"

The highest concentration of Japanese subs were in the Equatorial Pacific.

"All a Japanese sub captain had to do," said Marty, "was sit tight, and wait for our vain captain to come along, then nail it!"

After making its ceremonial crossing at the Equator and the Antemeridian, the troop carrier meandered around New Zealand, up through the northern coasts of Australia and New Guinea, before settling into Leyte Gulf. Allied forces had just invaded the Philippines, and were now in the "mopping up" phase of the Leyte Gulf naval battle. "We went to Base 17," said Marty, "that was in Samar"—the easternmost island province of the Philippines. "From there, I was waiting to be assigned to a boat."

After a few days, the personnel office told Marty that he'd be assigned to a new PT boat, sailing from the advance base on Borneo.

"Fine, I'm ready," he said.

When he got to Borneo, however, he was unwittingly placed upon the USS *Oyster Bay*—not a PT boat, but a "PT Boat Tender." In practice, the Tenders were floating logistical stations, responsible for carrying fuel and provisions to their designated PTs.

Still, the *Oyster Bay* had an illustrious combat history.

Marty Romano in his employee portrait for Edwards & Kelcey. As a civil engineer, Marty designed several prominent landmarks in Minnesota, including the Richard I. Bong Memorial Bridge.

"It was a converted destroyer," he said, whereas most Tenders were converted LSTs. "It had seen plenty of action—kamikaze attacks and all. Before I got there, they were involved in the Okinawa operation." But as a PT-rated engineer, Marty knew virtually nothing about the *Oyster Bay*'s propulsion system. Unlike the Packard-based powertrains aboard *PT-306*, the *Oyster Bay* was a double-shafted, diesel-powered vessel. Moreover, the ship's company already had a team of mechanics who were rated on the diesel powerplant; and they were doing a fine job of maintaining the *Oyster Bay*'s engine suite.

Thus, Marty had become an engineer with *no* engine to maintain.

The inopportune assignment, however, was short-lived. Days later, the US dropped its first atomic weapons over the Empire of Japan. Following the nuclear devastation of Hiroshima and Nagasaki, the Japanese government lost its will to fight.

Like many of his shipmates, Marty felt that the nuclear attacks ultimately saved more lives than they took. At the time, the *Oyster Bay* was being refitted for the invasion of Japan. And both sides were expecting a bloodbath. Some Japanese civilians were digging trenches along the beaches of Honshu, while others were being issued pitchforks to attack incoming paratroopers. But those fears never came to pass. For with the stroke of a pen, World War II finally ended on September 2, 1945.

Marty Romano was honorably discharged from the United States Navy on January 12, 1946. Under the terms of the newly-created "GI Bill," he enrolled at the Clarkson College of Technology (now Clarkson University) in New York. Inspired by watching the construction of the George Washington Bridge during his childhood, Marty enrolled in the Civil Engineering program, graduating with a Bachelor of Science degree in 1952. Meanwhile, as he approached his final semester in college, Marty married his longtime girlfriend, Lorraine, on September 15, 1951.

For the next 37 years, Marty was a proud employee of Edwards & Kelcey, a civil engineering and construction firm based in Morristown, New Jersey. A simple twist of fate, however, soon put Marty and his young family on the road to the American heartland. One morning, Edwards & Kelcey's Minneapolis office called in to the Morristown headquarters with a by-name request for "Marty Romano" - a top-flight structural engineer whom they needed for a series of projects in the Twin Cities. "They got a big job from the State of Minnesota," said Marty, "which included the Lowry Hill Tunnel." His by-name request had come via the office director at the Minneapolis branch, whom Marty had worked with on previous civil projects.

The Minnesota project was supposed to be a temporary assignment; but Marty, Lorraine, and their two daughters (Eileen and Joanne) soon made the North Star State their permanent home. Aside from the prominent Lowry Hill Tunnel, Marty went on to become the lead engineer for several high-profile infrastructure projects. Many of these structures have become prominent landmarks within the state of Minnesota. In addition to the Lowry Hill Tunnel, these projects included: the 11th Street South Bridge in Minneapolis; the Portland Avenue Tunnel in Minneapolis; and the Richard I. Bong Memorial Bridge connecting Duluth, Minnesota to Superior, Wisconsin. Marty retired from Edwards & Kelcey on December 29, 1989.

At this writing, Marty Romano is 97 years old, and still living an abundantly active life. He and Lorraine continue to reside in the Greater Minneapolis area.

3

BEHIND ENEMY LINES

KEN PORWOLL AND THE
BATAAN DEATH MARCH

The fires on Bataan burned with a primitive fury on the evening of April 9, 1942—illuminating the flags of surrender against the nighttime sky. Woefully outgunned, outnumbered, and ill-equipped, American-Philippine forces surrendered to the wrath of the Rising Sun. Some had escaped and eventually carried on as guerrillas. Most, however, like Sergeant Ken Porwoll, found themselves on the Bataan Death March.

Born on April 13, 1920 in St. Cloud, Minnesota, Ken Porwoll had no immediate draw to the military life. However, he joined the Minnesota National Guard in 1938 for reasons that had little to do with patriotism. "The National Guard sponsored a dance every New Year's, and it was the biggest social event of the winter," he said. "If you joined the Guard, you got a new uniform to wear to the dance." He saw the uniform as an opportunity to meet girls. "That was the incentive for three or four of us who signed up." Then, too, it was the middle of the Great Depression, and the extra monthly paycheck was a nice bonus.

Ken joined the National Guard as a tank crewman, assigned to the 34th Tank Company (later redesignated Company A, 194th Tank Battalion). At the time, the Minnesota Guard was on the verge of transitioning from the M2 Light Tank to the M3 Stuart. Both tanks, however, were thinly-armored, and neither had a particularly strong main gun. Still, Ken enjoyed learning how to operate the tanks, and he took readily to the life of a citizen-soldier. Even after World War II had officially started in Europe, Ken was certain that the war would never come to America. The Nazis were, after all, Europe's problem.

However, the 194th Tank Battalion was "federalized" in the fall of 1941—mustered into active service. A few weeks later, Ken and his comrades were on their way to Fort Lewis, Washington for additional training. In September of that year, the 194th received orders to the Philippine Islands. "All my life, I'd dreamed of going to the South Seas," he said. "Now, I'm going to get a free trip." He thought little of the war in Europe, and wasn't the least bit concerned about the Japanese. "Our only concern was getting our equipment clean. It was covered with that Marfak grease." His battalion arrived at Pier 7 in Manila Harbor on September 26, 1941—unloading 54 tanks for the convoy into Fort Stotsenberg in south-central Luzon.

An American Commonwealth since 1898, the Philippine Islands had enjoyed the full protection of the United States military. American forces in the Philippines fell under the jurisdiction of the United States Armed Forces—Far East (USAFFE). Commanded by an Army General, USAFFE encompassed all US military assets in the Philippine archipelago. This included American ground forces, the Far East Air Force, the Asiatic Fleet, and the semi-autonomous Philippine Army. USAFFE's mission was simple: continue providing combat-capable units for the Commonwealth's defense and assume responsibility for training the Philippine Army.

Despite these mission parameters, however, USAFFE remained in a deplorable state of combat readiness. In the midst of their isolationist fervor, Congress had straddled the US military with a draconian budget. As a result, USAFFE perennially subsisted on less than half of the money and equipment it needed for an adequate defense of the Philippines.

Upon arriving at Fort Stotsenberg, Ken discovered that there were no spare parts, no high-explosive tank ammunition, and minimal gasoline. To make matters worse, they had no extra ammunition for their M1 rifles. "When guards ended their watch, they'd pass their ammunition to the guy replacing them."

On the morning of December 8, 1941, Ken awoke to the news that Pearl Harbor had been bombed. That morning, "[our] tanks deployed around Clark Field," said Ken, moving into defensive positions against the incoming Japanese forces. "At about noon, we looked up, and saw a flight of planes coming over and said, 'Oh good, it's okay now because the Air Force is here'"—until those planes started dropping bombs. Ken said it was the first time in his military career that he felt truly helpless.

"What do you do?" he asked rhetorically.

From a tank, he couldn't shoot at the incoming bombs, and he couldn't traverse his main gun high enough to shoot down the incoming

Ken Porwoll as a POW. A member of the 194th Tank Battalion, Ken survived the Bataan Death March and a three-year internment at various POW camps.

planes. One hour later, Clark Field lay in ruins. "What wasn't blown up was on fire."

Company A was then ordered south into Muntinlupa to meet the anticipated Japanese landings. But when these landings came farther north, Ken's company had the unenviable task of turning northward to halt the enemy's advance—and the Japanese were already 30 miles inland. "When I came from Muntinlupa going north, we stopped at the Manila Hotel to get a drink, and the people in there were playing cards and having fun."

Ken could hardly believe it.

The Philippine Islands were under siege, and many of these Filipinos were carrying on as if nothing had happened. The cheerful Filipinos told Ken and his comrades: "Don't worry about it, boys. Uncle Sam will take care of these Japs. They'll never take Manila."

Ken wasn't so sure.

"You better get your walking shoes on," he told them. "And get out of town because they're coming and they'll be here." Yet these Filipinos paid no heed to his warning; such was their faith in the American military.

In the end, however, Company A was cut off, and had to make a hasty retreat. For a young tank sergeant like Ken Porwoll, the whole affair seemed like an exercise in futility. "All I can remember is running from one place to another with a tank," he said. Adding to the chaos was the growing blur between enemy and friendly lines. As the Japanese moved farther south, their positions became intermingled with the Allied defenders. For example, Sergeant Jim McComas, one of Ken's fellow tankers, inadvertently ran through a Japanese Command Post. During the ensuing chaos, a Japanese soldier tossed a thermite bomb onto the back of McComas' tank, "so that it burned a hole down through the armor and into the engine compartment; and got it so hot in the tank that some of the ammunition began to explode." The thermite fuse finally sank into the engine compartment, whereupon it disabled the tank. But miraculously, McComas survived.

Company A's retreat was cut short, however, when a group of nearby Filipinos heard the oncoming roar of American tanks and, mistaking them to be Japanese, blew up the local bridge in a panic. With no means of egress for their armored vehicles, Company A disabled and abandoned their tanks, rejoining the American lines on foot. To disable the tank, Ken said: "The only thing you could do was take the back plates off the guns, and throw them into the jungle someplace where they might not be found; and the guns become unusable."

When the remnants of Ken's battalion hobbled into Bataan, he was given command of another tank. Company A was then placed on coastal defense duty, firing on Japanese ships to prevent their landing. For a while, the American-Philippine forces were able to hold back the Japanese onslaught. But time was not on the Allies' side. The dwindling supplies and lack of reinforcements were beginning to take their toll. "As soon as we arrived [in Bataan], they put us on half rations," he said. "Then in February, they cut our rations again. They had armed guards on the chow wagons."

By now, disease was running rampant through the ranks.

Malaria began to claim more men than enemy gunfire. "They were out of Quinine, they were out of Atabrine, there was no mosquito netting," recalled Ken. "They didn't have anything." For the last two days of the battle, Ken survived on only one tin of sardines, which he shared with two of his friends. "We were so weak; it took three men to do one man's job."

Still, news of the Allied surrender came as a total surprise to him. "Runners came and told us we would be surrendered in the morning. They had us disable our tanks and disable our equipment."

Ken was incredulous; and some of his comrades refused to believe it.

"Well, I'm not going to surrender," they said.

They were determined to evade the Japanese and carry on the fight. But one of the officers said: "Well, if you don't surrender, that means you are deserting. You become a deserter and you will be court-martialed after the war." To some, however, a court-martial was better than becoming a POW. "And despite that threat, some of them still took off into the jungles," said Ken. Indeed, there was no legal basis to charge them for desertion as long as they continued fighting the enemy. In fact, many of these early American escapees—including Russell Volckmann, Robert Lapham, Wendell Fertig, and Charles Cushing—organized guerrilla movements against the Japanese. "My decision," said Ken, "was to stay with the group. What the group does, I will do."

The next day, April 10, the men of the 194th Tank Battalion assembled along a nearby road in the 100-degree heat. Before their departure, Ken recalled that one of the lieutenants opened the company treasury, dividing the money among the men. "And the cooks came with all the food they had left," he added, "dividing it out among the men and said: 'That's it. There is no more, guys.'" Awaiting the arrival of their conquerors, Ken didn't recall much anxiety among his comrades. Some seemed to think that the Japanese would treat them decently.

Those feelings would soon evaporate.

For when the first group of Japanese soldiers came through their area, Ken noticed that one of them was "real flushed...red in the face, as if he had a fever." The Japanese soldier collapsed, and his commanding officer, a Japanese lieutenant at the front of the column, quickly turned about, "unhitched his sword, and beat this man with the scabbard until the man got on his feet and walked off."

Ken was appalled.

If the Japanese did that to their own men, what would they do to the Americans?

When the Japanese got ahold of Ken and his fellow GIs, they took many of their personal belongings. "They picked our pockets. They took money, they took watches, they took rings. If a man had a ring they couldn't get off, they'd cut his finger off. If they found any item—a wallet, a comb—that had 'Japan' written on it, they killed the American on the spot. It meant you had taken it from a Japanese."

The Japanese then forced him to march some 65 miles to Camp O'Donnell. With 150 of his comrades, Ken made the grueling trek through the blazing heat with minimal food, water, and the constant threat of harassment from the Japanese. Some 12,000 Americans and 67,000 Filipinos were forced into this treacherous hike.

History would call it the Bataan Death March.

More than 7,000 would die along the way. "Anyone who lagged behind that first day was shot," said Ken. "After the first day, they just bayoneted you. They didn't think you were worth a bullet."

But for Ken Porwoll, the Death March was an intensely personal affair.

As National Guardsmen, most of the soldiers in Company A, 194th Tank Battalion were from the same hometown in Minnesota. It was a "very personal experience," he said, "in that I found myself walking with four other fellows that I had gone to high school with." They had played on the same football and basketball teams; they had competed for the same girls' affections; and they had grown up knowing each other's families. "You know almost everybody in the company," he added. In some ways, they drew strength from these bonds of familiarity—"and in another way," he said, "it's rather distressing too, when things get tough, and you have to make decisions as to who gets what...or who dies, who lives."

Ken hoped that he would never have to make that call. But his buddy, Jim McComas, who had survived the thermal charge aboard his tank during the invasion, came down with malaria on the second day of the Death March. Jim was a big, healthy man…and the fever didn't bother him at first. But when his fever devolved into a chill, he lost all control of his limbs. "So, we get one on either side of him," said Ken, "and helped drag him along the road." Ken and each of his friends took turns shouldering Jim. "We'd keep changing off about every hour or so until Jim said that we were going to have to drop him in the ditch because we won't make it if we have to carry him."

But Ken refused to leave his buddy.

"Let's keep trying a little while longer," he argued.

But Jim wouldn't have it.

"You've got to drop me in the ditch," he insisted.

By now, Jim knew that all the stragglers would be killed. "If you were beside the road when the column passed," Ken recalled, "the Japanese clean-up squad came by and killed you."

It was the horrible decision that Ken hoped he'd never have to make.

He and his friends knew they had to leave Jim behind.

"And I'm apologizing to him for our friendship coming to this kind of an end." But Jim McComas simply replied:

"Forget it, Ken. I'll just have to find another way."

With that, Jim crawled into the ditch, presumably leaving himself for dead. "We never spoke his name the rest of the walk. That was really tough."

For the next six days, Ken could hardly keep himself upright. The sweltering heat, humidity, and lack of nutrition were taking their toll. Moreover, he was astounded by the cruelty and barbarity of the Japanese Army. Some of the Japanese peeled the skin from their captives' feet, and forced them to walk through piles of salt. Other prisoners were deliberately run over by Japanese trucks racing at full speed. Yet, the most frightening stories were those of the Japanese eye gouging techniques: taking a rifle with a fixed bayonet, an enemy soldier would place the bayonet inside of a POW's bottom eyelid, and then let go of the rifle. Consequently, as the rifle fell to the ground, the bayonet would eject the prisoner's eye from his socket.

Aside from their astonishing cruelty, what angered Ken the most was the Japanese Army's casual, indiscriminate attitude towards its POWs. There was no rhyme or reason behind any of their methods. In fact, it seemed as though the Japanese were torturing Americans for their own amusement.

On the sixth day of the Death March, Ken found an opportunity. During a lull in the March, he spied a small pot cooking over a fire where a group of Japanese had bivouacked. Thinking that this abandoned pot might contain stew (or some other viable sustenance), he stealthily grabbed the pot and slipped back into the ranks of the Death March. After a few more paces down the road, he snuck a glance into the pot.

"I took off the lid and found that it was tea. That was a little disappointing."

Still, he happily shared it with the men around him. "We all had tea that afternoon." In his eight days on the Bataan Death March, Ken survived on nothing more than two handfuls of rice, two canteens of water, and a cup of tea.

The first stop on the Bataan Death March was the barbed-wire compound at San Fernando. "And the second morning I'm there...I look into the eyes of Jim McComas!"—the malaria-stricken GI whom they had presumed dead after he crawled into the roadside ditch.

Ken was ecstatic. "How did you get here?!"

"Well," said Jim, "when I went in the ditch and I looked up ahead, I saw a culvert, and I crawled into it and slept off the malaria attack. And the second day when another group of Americans came by, I crawled out and joined them."

Ken recalled that seeing Jim McComas, alive, helped restore some of his faith in God. He later confessed: "I was angry at God." In fact, he would often ask: "God, where are you; and what are you going to do about this?" On other occasions, particularly during the Death March, "I just hollered at Him," said Ken. But the second time he shouted at God, he heard a voice in the back of his head saying: "Ken, if you want to get to the end of this road, you have to walk it. So, you better focus on what your job is, and focus on walking. Stay attuned to what you have to do to get there." At the end of the Death March in San Fernando, Ken repented for his anger. "God, I'm sorry. You were there, weren't you? And you do care." But Ken admitted that, during the darkest days of his internment, he often vacillated between anger and gratitude—"every six months or so."

From San Fernando, Ken was among the many POWs crammed into the steel boxcars for the two-and-a-half-hour journey into Camp O'Donnell. "Men died of suffocation and from the heat...we were packed so tightly, there was no room to even fall down."

Camp O'Donnell itself was worse than the train ride.

Indeed, more than 400 Americans were dying every day at O'Donnell. "Burial details just went all day long. It never ended." To make matters worse, the camp was overcrowded and suffered from poor sanitation. "The water supply was one spigot that ran very slow," he said. "Too many people and not enough facility." The GIs who hoped that Camp O'Donnell would be a reprieve soon found otherwise. In fact, some of the prisoners who went to sleep that first night, didn't wake up in the morning. Some had died from malnourishment and exhaustion; some had died from their tropical diseases; while others simply committed suicide.

And the body count continued to rise.

As Ken recalled, many of his comrades were dying by the hour. Dysentery, malaria, beriberi, and a host of other diseases were running rampant through the camp. The "latrines" were nothing more than hastily-dug slit trenches, none of which were sanitized or had any type of drainage system. "And so, the flies moved in," he said—which inevitably carried fecal matter onto the prisoners' food. "And there were so many dying that there weren't enough [able-bodied] men to bury them, or to carry them to the burying grounds."

At one point, the Japanese began bribing POWs with extra rations of rice in exchange for burial duty. "They said whoever would work on the detail would get one and then two extra rations of rice," said Ken. Many of the POWs who accepted the deal, however, found that they simply couldn't bring themselves to bury their own comrades. When these POWs hesitated to throw their lifeless comrades into the mass graves, the Japanese simply threw the living POWs down into the graves as well...to be buried alongside their dead friends.

"The food was terrible," said Ken. POWs were normally given two rations of rice a day. But the Japanese deliberately overcooked it—"they boiled rice to a consistency of oatmeal...and they called it lugau." Getting water was also a hassle. A long queue of POWs formed by the water spigot every day; and the Japanese shut off the water at night. "So, you stood in line...because if you got out of line, you wouldn't get back into the same position you were in during the daytime."

After four weeks at Camp O'Donnell, Ken was unexpectedly transferred to Batangas—another prison camp where the POWs were placed on work details. "We were building a bridge over a gorge," he said. "In the beginning...I came down with yellow jaundice, and I was given the option of staying and doing light duty, or being sent back to O'Donnell." Without hesitation, Ken said: "I'll take the light duty." The piecemeal tradeoff for being at Batangas was that he received slightly better food and medical attention. "And my light duty was to carry water from a well that was about two and a half blocks away to the kitchen and the schoolyard where we were living."

For his lingering yellow jaundice, someone placed a one-pound bag of sugar by the well, with a note (written in English) that read: "Take three spoons each day. It will help with your yellow jaundice." Every few days, the one-pound bag of sugar would be replenished.

But who had left the bag there?

Ken never knew. "I never did see anybody. Or hear anybody."

Perhaps it was a sympathetic Filipino; or an altruistic Japanese soldier.

When he recovered from his yellow jaundice, however, he was thrust back into the realm of hard labor. Building that bridge, as he described it, was "really hard." Indeed, there were no automated tools—everything was done manually.

But, for what it was worth, this group of Japanese soldiers treated him better than the guards at O'Donnell. The Japanese officer-in-charge told his men that he would be the only one to administer punishment to a POW. "And so, they all understood that," said Ken. "And then he would give us the [same] rations that he gave his men, too."

Still, the Japanese were not gracious hosts.

Ken soon transferred to Cabanatuan, where he was given the mundane task of being a farm weeder. He stayed at Cabanatuan for three months before he was tapped for a work detail on the Japanese mainland. "I'm in this detail and I leave Cabanatuan," he remembered, "and I'm walking down the road and I need to take a leak." But as soon as he stepped out of line to relieve himself, he was attacked by two Japanese guards. With the butts of their rifles, they bashed Ken across the neck and the small of his back. "And I go tumbling in the ditch unconscious."

His handlers left him for dead. And Ken likely would have died by that roadside had it not been for the "cleanup squad" that came by a few minutes later—"a truck with American POWs on it picking up stragglers…they pick me up and throw me in the truck; and they take me to the railroad station." Once there, the Japanese loaded the POWs into boxcars for a short ride into Manila Bay. "Then, we get on a truck and I'm trucked to Pier Seven"—the very same dock where he had arrived with the 194th Tank Battalion months earlier. The Japanese intended to put this group of POWs on a ship to Japan, where they would likely take up hard labor in the mines or shipyards of Honshu or Hokkaido. But as he looked at the rusty old ship, he told himself:

"Ken, don't get on that ship. You'll die on that sucker."

Somehow, he was sure of that.

So, he crawled off behind some steel girders and went to sleep. When he awoke, the ship was gone and he was alone on the pier. Ken laid there until two Filipinos came passing by. He tried to convince them to provide food, or hide him temporarily. Normally, most Filipinos were happy to do so. But every war produces its own cadre of enemy collaborators—and this war was no different. Indeed, these two Filipinos came back a few minutes later with a pair of Japanese soldiers in tow. "I later learned," said Ken, "that they could get a hundred pesos for turning in an American."

The Japanese soldiers tried to make Ken walk, but given the condition of his health, he could barely stand. Frustrated, the Japanese tossed him onto a two-wheeled, horse-drawn carriage, and laid him across the reins, using Ken's body as a footrest as they took him to the POW camp in Bilibid. "They hammered on the gates until somebody opened them," he recalled, "and they have some conversation…then they leave…and take me to the execution chamber." They dragged him over to a cement block where an electric chair had once stood.

At first, Ken was certain that he was going to be killed.

But, as it turned out, he was just the newest resident of the prison's medical ward. It was the place where the Japanese sent POWs whom they considered terminally ill. As luck would have it, though, Ken met a familiar face in the crude medical ward—Jose Santos, a fellow trooper from the 194th Tank Battalion. Santos, however, was not a native Minnesotan. He had joined the 194th as a "replacement" when the battalion was at Fort Lewis. Santos helped nurse Ken back to health, slowly enabling the latter to regain his strength.

Ken was then sent back to Cabanatuan for three months, before he finally boarded a ship (Taga Maru) to Japan on September 20, 1943. The conditions onboard the ship, however, were no better than the POW camps. Describing the cargo holds: "They're so crowded, that you hardly have room for everybody to sit down at the same time. There were two [cargo] holds in this thing. Forward and the rear hold. The toilet was a washtub in the middle of the hold. There's no lid on it. And people that have diarrhea can't get to it anyway, because you have to walk on people to get there. And those that make an attempt, by the time they get there, they're all done. They don't need the tub anymore."

With the Taga Maru rocking back and forth along the waves, the prisoners' own fecal matter sloshed and sprayed around the cargo hold. "You end up living like rats in a sewer," he said, "awash in human feces." Every day, the Japanese lowered a single bucket of rice into the cargo hold, whereupon the ranking POW would have to ration out the contents to his fellow prisoners—"so that each man in that [cargo] hold got a dipper of rice." But, as Ken recalled, malnutrition was the least of their worries—looking at his fellow POWs, he could tell they were devolving into madness. "They're hungry. They're starved. They're crazy. They're out of their minds," he said.

Ken arrived in Japan in October 1943, where he would spend the next twenty-two months working in the Niigata coal mines. However, being a POW had taken a toll on his health; and he had trouble keeping pace in the coal yard. "I didn't know it then," he said, "but I had tuberculosis of the spine in three vertebrae. All I knew was that I was in a lot of pain."

All the while, he wondered how the war was going for the Allies.

He and his fellow POWs hadn't heard anything aside from the ever-present rumor mill, which changed from day to day.

Were the Allies winning?

Had the Americans recovered from Pearl Harbor?

What was happening in Europe?

He didn't know.

But, for now, his biggest concern was trying to stay alive.

He seemed to catch a break, however, when he noticed that one of his Japanese guards had a rosary...indicating that he was among Japan's Christian minority. Ken, a devout believer himself, also had a rosary; and he approached the Japanese guard hoping to find some common ground. At first, the guard hastily dismissed Ken, telling him to go away. The next day, however, Ken approached the guard a second time, showing his rosary.

Now, the guard seemed more receptive, but he told Ken to put away the rosary.

However, this chance encounter may have ultimately saved Ken's life. Indeed, the following day, Ken was run over by a minecart along the tunnel's inner track. He had been pushing his own minecart when it got stuck at a bend in the track—"and the cart behind me comes pushing, and slams into me; and my legs end up underneath it." Within moments, two Japanese handlers came running, separated the two minecarts, and "carefully take me out from underneath...and they examine me for broken bones." After determining that Ken had no injuries, his Japanese Christian friend reassigned him to an "easy job" working the coal chute levers.

"That's how I got through my one-and-a-half years in Japan," he said.

One day, in August 1945, the Japanese officers suddenly abandoned Ken's camp without warning. Apparently, there had been a massive bombing strike on the Japanese mainland.

No surprises here, Ken thought.

After all, the rumor mill had reported numerous fire bombings.

But this time something was different.

"Whatever this thing was," he said, "it was enough to send [these officers] off." A few days later, there came news of a second aerial attack, whereupon the Japanese noncommissioned officers (sergeants) vacated the camp, leaving only the privates to look after the POWs. With no direction from their commissioned or noncommissioned officers, the Japanese privates simply faded away.

Once Ken realized that all the Japanese sentries had abandoned their posts, he knew the war must have ended. The hungry POWs then raided the camp warehouse, drawing whatever food and provisions they could scavenge. "I think we fed ourselves for at least a week before the Air Corps found us and dropped supplies, clothing, and medicine." Soon thereafter, he discovered that the premature exodus of his Japanese handlers had been caused by the atomic bombs dropped on Hiroshima and Nagasaki.

"I still maintain that I was the only POW who was ever personally repatriated by his commander-in-chief." Indeed, Minnesota Governor Harold Stassen, came to Japan to coordinate the release of all Minnesota National Guardsmen held as POWs. "We were out of there [Niigata] two days after the Missouri docked." After his repatriation, Ken spent nearly a year in the hospital getting spinal fusions to treat his lingering tuberculosis.

Returning to civilian life, Ken married his wife Mary-Ellen in 1953, with whom he had nine children. Settling in St. Paul, Minnesota, he was a proud employee of Capitol Gears for nearly three decades. Inspired by his fellow veterans, Ken volunteered more than 5,000 hours at the Minneapolis VA Hospital; and volunteered countless additional hours to the Listening House of St. Paul. "People ask me all the time if I've forgiven the Japanese," he said during his later years. "I have. I really have. But I'll tell you, sometimes, I have to forgive them two or three times a month because it still recycles."

Ken Porwoll passed away on Veterans Day 2013, at the age of 93.

4

DAWN LIKE THUNDER

ED WENTZLAFF,
PEARL HARBOR SURVIVOR

O f the 335 men who survived the sinking of the USS *Arizona*, less than a handful were still living by the early 2000s. One of the last remaining survivors was Ed Wentzlaff, who by the age of 92, had already made arrangements to be buried with his comrades in Pearl Harbor. "My ashes will be interred on the *Arizona*," he said. "It only makes sense. I was on board for three years before she was sunk. That's where all my friends are."

Born in 1917, Ed was the third of nine children born to a saloon-operating family. Despite the Prohibition, Ed's family generated most of their income from selling illegal alcohol. And, as expected, the Wentzlaff family had numerous close calls with the federal Prohibition agents. "I remember saving my dad one time," he recalled. "I just happened to be out collecting for my paper route, when I saw this new big car coming into town. It had three guys in it."

But the car itself looked out of place, as did its occupants.

Typically, only federal agents conducted themselves in such a manner. "I raced home on my bike and told my dad, 'They're coming.' They were able to hide everything they had behind the bar before the agents got there."

After graduating from high school in 1935, Ed went to work for the Great Northern Railroad in Walker, Minnesota. Even during the midst of the Great Depression, Ed recalled: "I never had any trouble finding jobs because I always worked hard. I always believed in giving them their dollars' worth. The best job I had in those days was picking corn for $6.00 a day. That was big money in the 1930s." Indeed it was. When adjusted for inflation, his daily wages had the purchasing power of nearly $125 in today's money.

Ed worked a variety of farm and labor jobs throughout the Depression, but it was tough getting ahead. "I got disgusted about always being poor," he admitted. "A friend of mine had joined the Navy earlier that year, and then another friend joined up. For some reason, I decided I would too."

For a young man growing up in the Great Depression, the Navy seemed like a good way to make a living. Sailors got free uniforms, free meals, endless opportunities for travel, and the chance to learn a technical trade that could carry over into the private sector.

Ed Wentzlaff enlisted in the United States Navy on December 8, 1937. He completed boot camp at Great Lakes Naval Training Station in Chicago; then it was off to the Naval Ordnance School in San Diego, learning about the common variety of naval weapons. Ed was fascinated by the concept of torpedoes, and requested duty aboard a submarine. "But, of course, this was the Navy," he said, "and they sent me to a battleship."

That battleship was the USS *Arizona*.

When Ed reported to the *Arizona* in 1938, he first worked as a cook and pot-scrubber. It was the job that often befell new sailors when they reported to the ship. For many, it was considered a "rite of passage," before joining the ship's functional crew. After several months in the mess galley, however, Ed joined the ordnance crew on the *Arizona*'s forward gun batteries. He was now officially a "gun striker"—maintaining the black powder magazines below deck.

In mid-1939, however, there came an opening for an ordnance mate aboard one of the *Arizona*'s scout planes. "Everybody wanted to fly those planes," Ed recalled. The OS2U Kingfisher seaplane could be launched from the deck of any battleship, and recovered by a shipboard crane after landing on the sea. Ed won the coveted Kingfisher assignment through a combination of good luck and steady mentorship. With the help of an officer who had taken a liking to him, Ed was able to qualify as an Aviation Ordnance Mate Third Class, and found himself at the top of the recommendation list for the scout plane assignment.

Over the next few years, the USS *Arizona* shifted her home port from California to Pearl Harbor. In the years immediately prior to December 7, the ship spent most of its time at sea. In port, however, Ed recalled that the *Arizona* had a tremendous recreation program—"good baseball teams, football teams, wrestling, you name it. The crew spent all of its time together." Because the *Arizona* was a flagship, it also hosted a rear admiral, Isaac Kidd. "He was one of the orneriest admirals in the fleet," Ed remembered. "Everybody hated him. Our airplanes were on the

Ed Wenztlaff. The son of a bootleg saloon owner, Ed joined the Navy as a means to escape the Great Depression. He requested duty aboard a submarine, but was given a billet aboard the USS *Arizona*.

quarterdeck, and the admiral considered the quarterdeck his territory. He made us do all our work in dress whites. You tell me—how do you change the oil on an airplane in your dress whites?"

Grumpy admirals notwithstanding, Ed enjoyed his job on the *Arizona*; and he rose quickly through the ranks. In September 1941, he had passed the test to become an Aviation Ordnance Mate First Class. But the promotion itself would have to wait—"there were no first-class slots available at the time." Still, his duties aboard the Kingfisher aircraft remained the same: he took care of the plane's onboard weapons—"including the machine gun and bomb racks." As it turned out, maintaining the aircraft's machine gun was a daunting task. Just like the World War I biplanes, the Kingfisher's machine gun fired *through* its propeller. Thus, Ed became an expert at "synchronizing the machine guns so they wouldn't shoot off the plane's propeller." As an Aviation Ordnance Mate, Ed was also rated as part of the air crew, for which he drew flight pay.

December 7, 1941 began as a joyful day for Ed Wentzlaff. His four-year enlistment in the Navy was scheduled to end the following day. He and another friend were planning to leave the Navy and open a resort in Wisconsin. "It was a beautiful morning," he said. "As usual, I got up early to take a shower while there was still hot water, so I was probably up a half-hour before reveille. Just before 8 o' clock, I was up on the forecastle waiting for service to begin. I was Catholic, but they were having Lutheran service on our ship because the chaplain was Lutheran. They were just setting up the chairs. There were about 12 of us."

A few minutes before 8:00 AM, Ed looked out over the Harbor and saw an incoming airplane. "I could see the red ball on its side. It was coming right down the line of ships and strafing as it came. When it got to us, the bullets were hitting the teak wood on deck, and the wood and splinters were flying all over. Someone told us to get below. There was a kind of rule in the Navy that a ship was bombproof if you got down to the third deck."

But today, the *Arizona* would tragically disprove that theory.

On his way down to the lower decks, Ed roused a few of his shipmates from their sleep. "I told them they should get below," but his sleepy-eyed comrades refused to believe that the attack was real. They insisted that it was just the Army Air Corps simulating another attack; and that the Army staged these simulations regularly. "I told them to look out the porthole, and they'd see it wasn't a simulation."

Ed continued following his shipmates through the lower decks, down

The USS *Arizona* in 1931, after completing her upgrades and modernization.

to "what was thought to be an impregnable part of the ship." But as he approached the final ladder, he changed his mind. "I was the last one in the group," he remembered, "and they all went down below and I didn't." For some reason, Ed couldn't bring himself to hide in the bowels of the ship. "I don't know why I didn't follow them down there; I don't know. But my General Quarters station was up on the quarterdeck. Damn, don't you know, I just turned around and went back up."

That decision probably saved his life.

"There were some fires on the deck already, and a lieutenant commander told us to grab a fire hose. We got it out, and I told the other guy to stay at the valve until I was ready at the other end of the hose. When I had a good grip on it, I told him to hit the water, but nothing happened. I thought he might have opened the wrong valve, so we changed places and I tried to open the valve. But there was no water. We had already been torpedoed by that time."

As Ed was trying to open the valve, a Japanese Zero dropped its bomb through the upper decks of the *Arizona*, setting off the powder magazine at the forward edge of the ship. Most of the *Arizona*'s forward section disappeared in that horrific blast. "I was protected a little bit," he said, "but it burned off all my hair, my eyebrows." A nearby Marine had fared even worse. He was the commander of the ship's Marine detachment and, as Ed recalled: "he had a huge chunk missing on his forehead, and another chunk missing on his cheek." Yet this fatally-wounded Marine kept yelling, "We're going to get those SOBs!" until he expired a few moments later.

"Someone was yelling to abandon ship, but when I looked over the side, and saw all that oil burning, I didn't know if I wanted to jump into that. If I had jumped, I don't think I would have made it to shore." Thus, Ed and another sailor ran to the officer's gangway, where the admiral's barge was tied. Although the *Arizona* was sinking, the barge's line was still taut.

The sinking battleship was taking the barge down with her.

Ed yelled to the other sailor: "If you can get the engine going, I'll cut us loose!" Ed tried his three-inch blade on the mooring rope, but it was no use. "I went in the admiral's cabin and I found a flag staff that he used for official ceremonies. It had a metal device on the top of it, and I brought that out and started hacking at the line. I finally got it parted."

The other sailor got them underway. "We went down the side of the ship, and there was a group of men, they were just black from head to foot," Ed recalled. "So many men were burned, and they were burned all over because all they had on when the ship exploded were their shorts [skivvies]. We got them on board the barge, and brought them over to the hospital ship in the harbor, the USS *Solace*. If any of them lived, it had to be a miracle."

Ed spent the next several hours going in and out of Battleship Row, picking up survivors wherever he could find them. At one point, he ferried a group of badly-burned sailors to the onshore Navy Hospital.

"All those guys wanted were cigarettes," he recalled.

Somehow, these wounded sailors preferred nicotine over morphine.

"We hauled them over to the hospital, but there was no room inside, and we just had to put them on the lawn. The doctors would come around...but if you didn't look like you were going to make it, they just didn't bother." Indeed, these Navy doctors had to make the painful decision to bypass the fatally-wounded, and focus their energies on those who *could* be saved.

Moreover, Ed was astounded by how quickly the chain of command had broken down after the opening shots. "On the *Arizona*, nearly all of the senior officers were killed in the blast," including the maligned

The *Arizona* burns after being struck by Japanese bombs during the attack on Pearl Harbor.

Admiral Isaac Kidd. "We were all orphans out there," Ed remembered. "In fact, there was no command at all."

Still, Ed tried to help wherever he could.

At one point, he found himself on the USS *West Virginia*, as part of an ad hoc team desperately trying to save the ship. They knew they couldn't stop the ship from sinking, but they wanted to save it from capsizing. For if the ship could sink straight down, the Navy might have a chance to salvage it. "I remember talking to one guy who served on the *West Virginia*," Ed recalled. "He was a friend of mine. He said that he had been ordered to flood some compartments, but he refused to do it because he knew some of his shipmates were in those compartments. They made him do it. He had to kill them. A month later, he was dead [from suicide]. He never recovered from that." Later in the day, Ed joined a group of servicemen digging gun pits along the shore. The Americans were certain that the Japanese would launch a second wave, and that an invasion of Oahu was on its way.

By nightfall, Ed and the other survivors had been hoarded into the shipyard, where they spent the night in the naval base recreation building.

"They gave us a rifle, some ammunition, a blanket, soup and a sandwich. We painted all the windows black." Around this time, however, these shell-shocked survivors committed their first case of fratricide. A group of planes from an American carrier flew over Pearl Harbor that evening. Ironically, these carriers had been the primary target for the Japanese High Command when planning the attack on Pearl. Fortunately, the carriers had been away on maneuvers that morning. But when these carrier-borne planes appeared over the devastated remains of Pearl Harbor, the spooked survivors opened fire. "We thought they were Japanese," Ed lamented, "and we were all firing at them with rifles and everything else we had. We shot five of them down. Two of the pilots were killed. We felt terrible. But that's just how it was that day. For a while, I was carrying two .45s in my belt."

Two days later, Ed and the other survivors were taken to the local Post Office. "We were allowed to send a post card saying: 'I am okay, and I will write later.' There was an officer with us to make sure that's all we wrote. My parents were first informed that I was 'missing in action,' and that was the truth. Nobody knew where anybody was."

After the attack on Pearl Harbor, Ed Wentzlaff knew he couldn't leave the Navy. The country was at war; and he had witnessed the opening shots. He remained on active duty for another four-and-a-half years. He served in a variety of postings throughout the war, including a temporary stint on the USS *Yorktown* before its sinking at Midway. While fighting the Japanese, Ed continued to rise through the ranks, and had become a chief warrant officer by the war's end.

Rather than become a career sailor, however, Ed returned to his native Minnesota. "For a year, I just relaxed and drank," he said. Given the horrors of combat, one could hardly blame him. It would take time to decompress from the psychological traumas of war.

Although America emerged victorious from World War II, many veterans and social commentators have criticized the War Department's lack of attention to the long-term psychological health of its servicemen. These men, like those who fought before them, suffered the long-term effects of "battle fatigue" (a condition that has since been rebranded as "Post-Traumatic Stress Disorder"); and there were no effective care or rehabilitation systems to help them re-integrate into postwar America. They were left largely to their own devices. Perhaps tacitly, these veterans were expected to find catharsis in the fact that they'd *won* the war and had defeated the forces of Fascism.

Ed later attended law school at the University of Minnesota; but the large classes, pompous professors, and lack of personal attention quickly turned him off to the legal profession. Instead, he turned to farming, a career that he held for the next 38 years. He also ventured into local politics, serving as the Mayor of Butterfield, Minnesota (west of St. Paul) and later became the Watowan County Commissioner.

Throughout his life, Ed found comfort in attending the various Pearl Harbor reunions with his surviving shipmates. He also travelled with a panel of World War II veterans, discussing their experiences at various venues across America. "There was one guy who was on the *Indianapolis*," he said. The USS *Indianapolis* was torpedoed by a Japanese submarine on July 30, 1945, resulting in the greatest loss of life suffered by a single American ship. "They [the panel] billed us as being on the first ship that was sunk [Ed on the *Arizona*] and the last ship that was sunk [the sailor from the *Indianapolis*] during the war."

And like many survivors, Ed Wentzlaff cast a critical eye on the Hollywood renditions of Pearl Harbor. He recalled *Tora! Tora! Tora!* as one of the best representations of the event. He also visited the USS *Arizona* Memorial at least eight times before his death. "I just look at all the names," he said. "There were so many good friends of mine."

In the twilight of his life, Ed reflected heavily on being one of the last living survivors from the Arizona. "I can't explain why I've lived so long," he said. "It's like the good Lord is saying: 'I'm going to keep him here until he gets it straightened out.'"

Ed Wentzlaff passed away on September 11, 2013.

True to his intentions, his ashes were interred aboard the USS *Arizona* during a commemorative ceremony on December 7, 2013. Seventy-two years after witnessing the attack on Pearl Harbor, Ed Wentzlaff had finally rejoined his 1,200 shipmates in their place of immortality.

5
AMERICAN SPITFIRE

FLOYD "ROD" RODMYRE,
USAAF SPITFIRE PILOT

Few Americans can claim to have flown a Supermarine Spitfire—the crown jewel of the RAF's Fighter Command. Lieutenant Floyd "Rod" Rodmyre was one of those lucky few. "A lot of people think it was the best fighter made by any country in World War II," he said. "I know what it was built for; it was perfection."

Growing up on a farm near Hector, Minnesota, Rod Rodmyre enjoyed the simple routines of Midwestern life. One of his most memorable childhood moments was the day a local resident started a school bus service. "My mom was so elated because it meant I'd get home from school in time to help out around the farm," he said. But, for as well-intentioned as this bus entrepreneur may have been, his vehicle of choice seemed to be a deathtrap. "It was built on a Ford Model A axis," Rod remembered. "The exhaust pipe fed into another pipe that ran through the length of the bus. That was our heater."

Graduating from high school in 1939, Rod attended Augsburg College for two years. Following the attack on Pearl Harbor, Rod approached his father, who was serving on the local draft board. "We had a little heart-to-heart," said Rod. "I asked him what my chances were [of being drafted], and he said I'd be the first to go." Rod was now 21 years old, in good health, and had no criminal record. Thus, he was a prime candidate for being classified "1A" for the draft.

In February 1942, Rod enlisted in the Army air cadet program. "But the way the military was in those days," he said, "they just sent us home on vacation." Indeed, the Army did not yet have enough airfields to accommodate the influx of new cadets. "So, I just collected my $30 a month at home."

But this homestead vacation wouldn't last long.

Barely one month later, he was recalled to Minneapolis and put on a train to Randolph Field, Texas. "We got on the train, and they put us in sleeping cars. I thought this was pretty nice and assumed that everyone got the same treatment. Later, I found out it was because we were air cadets, and we were future officers, so they were treating us like officers."

For the young Cadet Rodmyre, however, Flight School was a challenge like none other. "We went through a series of check rides, and I was not doing well. I took the first check ride and I flunked, and the second check ride and I flunked that. It didn't look good."

Failing two consecutive check rides had put him on notice with the flight instructors.

"I assumed I didn't have much chance to make number three, and so I figured it would be my last flight in the Army. I was as relaxed as an old shoe. I had given up completely; it was kind of shameful." But, that level of relaxation seemed to help his performance. He flew this third check ride without incident and made a picture-perfect landing. "We got out of the plane," he said, "and the officer...looked at me and said, 'Cadet Rodmyre, I don't know why I'm doing this, but I think I'm going to let you go on.' I almost gave him a hug," he laughed. "From that time on, I never had any problems in the air. I started acting like I had some potential." His hard work paid off; Rod earned his wings in November 1942. "Nothing I had done in my lifetime up to that date could compare with the feeling of accomplishment, pride, and happiness."

He then received orders to attend fighter training in Oakland, California. "That was another experience," he said. "It seems our flight commander didn't have much to do except drink. But, of course, the sergeants ran the place, and they got us into our training schedule." Throughout the course, Rod piloted the P-39 Airacobra. "We thought it was a wonderful plane," he said. "It had the tripod gear, and you could almost land it blindfolded. And, unlike our training planes, this one could actually shoot bullets." The P-39 itself had somewhat of a checkered reputation among the Allied air forces. Although the plane was easy to handle, it was typically derided among the Western Allies for its poor combat record.

Because he was on a West Coast training station, Rod anticipated being sent to the Pacific. Instead, his entire training class received bulk orders to Fort Dix, New Jersey, and soon found themselves on a troop carrier to England. "But after a few days at sea," he noted, "the weather was getting warmer. That shouldn't happen if we're going to England."

As it turned out, they had been diverted to North Africa.

"That was a serious change. All the nylons the guys had bought for the women in England were now excess baggage," he chuckled. Soon, the official announcement came that they were headed to Casablanca. "We were all joking that we would see Humphrey [Bogart] there." The real-life Casablanca, however, bore little resemblance to the soiree setting of Rick's Café. "It was hot," Rod remembered, "and it was stinky." The young pilots then took a bus some 30 miles to the Moroccan town of Berrechid. "You didn't have to slur your words too much to make it sound like something else."

Arriving at the airfield, however, Rod was puzzled to find British Spitfires—"the fighter plane that many credited with winning the Battle of Britain"—branded with American roundels and markings. Rod soon discovered that these Americanized Spitfires had been escorting P-39s on various missions over the Mediterranean. "We wondered about that," said Rod. "Fighters being escorted by fighters." At first, it didn't make sense. "It soon dawned on us that our P-39 wasn't much of a fighter plane."

Rod had been assigned to the 308th Fighter Squadron, 31st Fighter Group. "It was one of the best-known groups in the war," and was the first American air group to arrive in England in 1942. However, because their planes were deemed inferior to the German fighters, the Yankee pilots had swapped most of their P-39s and P-40s for Spitfires.

A few days later, Squadron headquarters asked for any volunteers interested in flying the Spitfire. "We looked at each other for about three seconds, and then it was a mad rush to sign up," said Rod. The volunteers were assigned to an RAF officer, Major Rusty Gates, who had fought in the Battle of Britain, and was now training Yanks to pilot the Spitfire. "He had a real Cockney accent," Rod remembered. "He told us everything about the Spitfire."

Of course, the Spitfire was much different from the American planes.

"The most significant difference was that everything was run by air pressure [i.e., pneumatics], including the firing of the guns."

Still, Rod was happy to be flying the Spitfire. "We realized that our life expectancy had just increased many-fold. It was such an easy plane to fly, it felt like it became part of you. We had a stupid grin on our faces for days." But the Spitfire wasn't the only piece of British equipment they were using. In fact, it seemed that the entire 308th Squadron had been equipped by His Majesty's armed forces. "We had RAF helmets, life vests, parachutes, boots, overalls, you name it."

Moreover, Rod was impressed by the cool nonchalance and derring-do of RAF pilots like Rusty Gates. For example, near the end of a training flight, Gates was on final approach when Rod spied a group of camel riders crossing the runway. "Gates just cruised in like nothing was there," Rod recalled, "and his landing wheel hit one of the camel drivers in the head…killed him instantly." Naturally, an irate Army Air Forces officer soon confronted Gates about the runway casualty.

Gates simply replied: *"By jove, I thought I felt a bump there."*

"I later learned," said Rod, "that the government gave $25 to the family of the camel driver. Life in wartime is very cheap."

In July 1943, Rod flew his first combat missions during the Invasion of Sicily. The 308th Fighter Squadron arrived in Sicily on D–Day+4, and began flying missions in support of Allied ground operations. The rules of flying in combat suddenly became real. "There wasn't any horseplay, or any useless radio chatter," he said. "There were two main commands. One was 'break right' and the other was 'break left.' Our squadron's radio name was 'Helpful.' So, you'd hear on the radio, 'Helpful, break right,' and you'd make this sudden, almost violent turn to the right," vectoring themselves into the direction of an enemy formation.

The Americans would maintain their tactical formations for as long as they could. "But once the dogfighting began, it was a mass of swirling planes, turning, diving, climbing, sometimes upside down," he said. "The dogfights rarely lasted more than a minute or two, but it seemed like an hour."

Still, the Spitfire held up remarkably well in a dogfight.

One of its few drawbacks, however, was its line of sight. "When it was on the ground, it was impossible to see straight ahead because of the angle of the plane." As Rod remembered: "For that reason, you always saw Spitfire pilots zig-zagging down the runway so they could look out the side windows and see what was in front of them."

At times, however, it seemed that the Spitfire jocks had more to fear from Allied vessels than enemy planes. During one mission, for example, Rod's flight was fired upon by an American cruiser off the northern coast of Sicily. Luckily, there were no casualties; but the encounter left him shaken. "I guess the rule was: 'If you can't identify it, shoot it down.' We got out of his range as fast as we could and continued patrolling."

As the Allied troops moved forward, so too did the airmen, "jumping from one airfield to another." But life on the airfield was by no means easy. Pilots would go for days without a shower or a change of clothes. "We would stuff our mattresses with wheat straw, so of course we got lice," said Rod. "We learned that we could soak our mattresses and clothes in

Floyd Rodmyre poses in front of his Americanized Spitfire. Rodmyre was one of the American few pilots in history to fly a Spitfire in combat.

aviation gas, and that would get rid of the lice."

The aviation gas could not, however, stave off malaria—which Rod contracted during his first few weeks in Sicily. "First the chills, then the fever, then the chills again," he said. "When I had the chills, they could put seven wool Army blankets on me and I'd still be shaking. When I had the fever, I was just sweating all the time." Still, his fellow pilots never missed an opportunity to inject their own dark humor into the healing process. For instance, Rod's friend, Les Schult came to his bedside with an accordion. "He sat down on the next bunk and played every funeral song he knew, and then left without saying a word."

Rod yelled after him: "I'm going to get well just so I can kill you!"

While stationed in Sicily, Rod also had a chance encounter with General George Patton. "I was walking past this bombed-out hangar where the walking-wounded troops were being cared for," Rod remembered. "Walking-wounded" referred to any wounded soldier who was still ambulatory. "All of a sudden," he continued, "Patton's car came roaring up with all the stars on the fender and the red flags flapping. I stood at frozen attention, hoping that he would just think I was a statue."

By now, Patton's reputation preceded him wherever he went. His bombastic and larger-than-life persona had won him several admirers (and enemies) throughout the Army. And today, the young Lieutenant Rodmyre would see Patton's colorful antics on full display. "The Jeep passed the hangar," he continued, "and then stopped and backed up at about 30 miles an hour. I didn't think Jeeps could go that fast in reverse. And out came Patton and he went into the hangar."

Rod braced himself for the tirade he knew was coming.

"He used every cuss word in the vocabulary of a whole division, and far more," Rod recalled. "He didn't seem to think the men were dressed right." The wounded soldiers hastily (and perhaps reluctantly) pulled their uniforms over their casts and bandages. Patton, eyeing the spectacle before him, said: "Now you look like soldiers. I'm proud to lead you, and I salute you."

The verbose General then saluted his troops, and stormed off in his Jeep.

Rod remembered that this hangar visit was only a few days before the infamous "slapping incident" with a shell-shocked GI...the incident that nearly derailed Patton's career.

As the action moved onto the Italian mainland, the 31st Fighter Group followed. The Spitfire jocks stayed at various airbases, following the path of Allied ground forces as they pushed the Germans farther north. For this portion of the Italian campaign, Rod and his wingmen often flew bomber escort missions, accompanying B-17s and B-24s on their various runs. But even the most aggressive fighter escorts couldn't prevent the occasional loss of a heavy bomber.

"When a [B-17] got hit, he usually made it back to base. But when those [B-24s] got hit. *Oy-yoy-yoy.* I saw one get hit, and watched four guys get out, but then the plane went into a spin and the centrifugal force kept anyone else from bailing out. I know the B-24 had a great reputation with some people, but nobody asked me." Indeed, heavy bomber crews had among the lowest life expectancies of any Allied personnel in the ETO.

Of course, Rod had his own near-brushes with death. During one mission, while serving as the flight leader's wingman, Rod felt a sudden jolt that rendered him unconscious. "All of a sudden, everything went black," he said. "I didn't know where I was. I was out, and when I came to, my plane was at about 6,000 feet in a very steep dive, going very fast." Jerking back on the stick, he pulled the Spitfire out of its dive just moments before hitting the ground. When he returned to base, however, the ground crew pointed to an 11x16-inch hole in his canopy.

He had been hit by a German bandit.

"The fragments of the shell had penetrated my leather helmet and entered my scalp," he said. "The other guys said I was talking gibberish on the radio before I came to." The flight surgeon removed the shrapnel from Rod's scalp, and he was flying the next day.

By this time, Rod Rodmyre had flown dozens of missions, but had yet to down an enemy fighter. "It seemed like most of the time in air battles, the enemy was shooting at me, and not the other way around," he lamented.

However, his fortunes changed on January 29, 1944.

"It was a one-on-one deal with a Focke-Wulf 190," he recalled. "We got going round and round, but I could out-turn him…I was making my turns as sharp as I could without stalling. Eventually, I came up behind him. He tried to out-dive me, but he had used up all his altitude. I just went after him and got him." Rod's victory was quite impressive given the reputation of the Fw 190. It was among the fastest and most powerful fighters in the *Luftwaffe*, but the Mark V Spitfires (and their latter-day variants) could easily out-turn the Focke-Wulf at lower and medium altitudes.

Eventually, the 308th received an upgraded variant of the Spitfire, and the pilots were finally given permission to name their planes. His friends chose a variety of colorful nicknames, but Rod prophetically nicknamed his crate the "Flying Viking"—a seemingly clairvoyant nod to the future Minnesota Vikings football team. "I was twenty years ahead of the football team in picking that name," he chuckled.

In March 1944, Rod's fighter group was transferred to the 15th Air Force. "It meant more spit and polish," he said, "but the barracks were better and the food was better." Indeed, he no longer had to contend with lice, straw mattresses, or the lingering smell of gasoline-soaked linens. "And there was one other major change: The group was assigned the American P-51 Mustang fighter to replace the Spitfires."

It was quite possibly the last news he wanted to hear.

"They called us all together in a big tent and told us we had to give up our Spitfires. We were just incredulous. We knew we were flying the best airplane in the world. We didn't think any American plane was as good." Given their experiences with the P-39 and P-40, one could hardly blame them.

But, as they soon found out, the P-51 Mustang was in a class all its own. It was fast, nimble, and could stand toe-to-toe against any Axis fighter. "It could fly for hours, whereas the Spitfire could only go an hour or an hour-and-a-half." Before long, Rod and his fellow pilots realized that the P-51 was "quite an airplane."

Still, the P-51's performance metrics couldn't save it from a pilot's bad judgement. Such was the case in the fall of 1944, when Rod was flying wingman for Les Schult, the flight leader of a four-plane formation. "There was some fighting," said Rod, "but it was not compelling, and we were headed home."

On the way back, however, Rod's radio died.

"I pulled alongside Les and indicated by tapping on my headphones that my radio wasn't working. So, I formed up on his wing. He was going to have to fly for both of us."

One of the other pilots in their formation, however, was about to make a fatal mistake.

This other pilot, whom Rod identified as a "goofball," saw a flight of enemy bombers below, and dove after them—"without checking the surrounding skies or letting Les Schult, the formation leader, know what was happening." Rod and Les reluctantly dove after the wayward wingman, trying to give him some top cover. "And of course, as he approached the bombers," said Rod, "the [Bf 109s] sprung the trap."

The "goofball" pilot was immediately shot down, and the remaining P-51s came face-to-face with *nine* German Messerschmitt fighters. "It just went on and on," said Rod. "It was probably a 15-minute air battle, but it seemed like hours...and I was staying on Les' wing. I was kind of useless without the radio."

Luckily, Les Schult and Rod Rodmyre escaped the melee and landed safely at their base. But the surprise dogfight had taken its toll on Rod. "I taxied to the parking spot and started to walk to Operations. All of a sudden, I couldn't walk anymore. My knee was shaking too badly. It was the only time I ever experienced that, and boy was it shaking."

Rod was showing the first signs of "battle fatigue."

Later, when the ground crew inspected Rod's plane, they discovered that two of his exhaust pipes had completely melted off. "And there was no gas, not one drop, left in the plane. I don't even know how I taxied in." He must have been running on fumes. "It was the closest thing to a miracle I've ever felt."

Whenever a pilot returned from a brutal mission like Rod Rodmyre's, the flight surgeons would often give them a fifth of whiskey. Although the libation was *technically* prohibited while in theater, flight commanders often looked the other way. Most pilots knew from experience that a quick shot of alcohol (in any form or fashion) could quiet their nerves and slow their adrenaline after a painful mission. Rod had little tolerance for alcohol, but he often took solace in nicotine, as did many of his peers. "I smoked incessantly," he said. "Cigarettes were free. Even the Red Cross girls were handing them out." Elsewhere on the frontlines, American GIs were typically rationed two cigarettes per soldier, alongside their typical C and K-Rations.

Finally, after completing 130 missions, Rod was summoned to the flight surgeon's office. "He told me that I was showing signs of fatigue, and that I was losing weight. I went to the Isle of Capri for some R&R." Upon his return, Rod Rodmyre flew an additional 30 sorties, bringing his combat mission tally to 160, whereupon he was ordered to take more R&R. "They said they were going to send me home for 90 days' rest."

Rod presumed the Army Air Forces would send him back to Europe, or maybe to the Pacific so he could diversify his combat experience. However, by this point in the war, the Army had churned out so many pilots that Rod was no longer needed on the frontlines. Thus, Rod Rodmyre finished the war stateside, as an instructor pilot for the P-47 Thunderbolt.

After the war, most of his friends continued to fly as commercial aviators. Rod, however, chose to hang up his wings. After his discharge from the US Army, he never flew again. "I had flown the best fighter planes of World War II, and any other flying would be boring." Returning to Minnesota, he finished college on the GI Bill. During that time, an old childhood friend introduced him to Miss Margaret Boehmlehner, whom he married in 1948.

Rod began his professional, post-war career in the home appliance industry. After 38 years, he retired as a senior manager at the Whirlpool Corporation. Both before and after his retirement, Rod remained an active volunteer in his community. He devoted several hours to the Pilgrim Lutheran Church in Minneapolis, serving on its School Board and mentoring its Boy Pioneers program. He also served on the Board of

Regents at St. Croix Lutheran High School.

Floyd "Rod" Rodmyre passed away on September 17, 2014 at the age of 92. He was the last surviving American Spitfire pilot.

6
EYEWITNESS NORMANDY

PARATROOPER JIM CARROLL RECALLS THE D-DAY INVASION.
JUNE 6, 1944.

J im Carroll was an unlikely hero. A native Minnesotan, he joined
the Army after he and three friends had seen a movie about
paratroopers. Fascinated by the concept of parachute infantry, Jim
and his buddies decided to visit the Army recruiter the following Monday.
It was November 1942, and the US had been at war for nearly a year. "I
got to where we were supposed to meet," Jim recalled—but his friends
were nowhere to be found. "I was the only one who showed. I guess the
rest of them had a change of heart over the weekend." He thus went to
the recruiting station alone.

The next day, Jim was sent to Jefferson Barracks in St. Louis, Missouri
where, not surprisingly, he spent his first day in the Army peeling potatoes.
It was the stereotypical, mundane task that often befell new recruits and
unlucky privates. It wasn't long, however, before he found himself in
Basic Training and Jump School at Camp Toccoa, Georgia. To earn the
coveted jump wings, he had to make five qualifying parachute jumps
from a C-47 at an altitude of 1,300 feet. Lining up along the inside of
the fuselage, Jim and his fellow paratroops would hook their "static lines"
to an overhead wire that ran the length of the plane. The static line was
generally a fifteen-foot cord attached to the parachute on a trooper's
back. Once the trooper jumped from the plane, the static line would
extend until taught, at which point it would deploy the parachute from
its pack as the trooper continued falling towards the ground.

"The first one was the easiest one," he said, "because I didn't know
what was happening." Still, that first jump was a nerve-racking experience
because the jumper in front of him broke his leg upon hitting the drop
zone. "I could hear his leg snap when it hit the ground," said Jim. "I could
hear it crack. That made me tense up a little bit."

Jim was assigned to the 501st Parachute Infantry Regiment, 101st Airborne Division. The regiment spent most of 1943 training at Camp Mackall and conducting maneuvers in Tennessee. "I remember one time, everybody's paycheck was shortened 11 cents," he said. "They told us later it was to pay the farmer back for the chickens we [the regiment] stole. I never even got a smell of those chickens." That November, Jim's regiment was sent to Boston and loaded onto a transport to England. "I was seasick every day," he recalled. "I've always had trouble with motion sickness and it was a rough crossing." Soon, however, Jim and the rest of the 501st, were camped at Newberry, England, where their training intensified. They were preparing for the invasion of mainland Europe. Nearly every day, Jim and his fellow paratroopers had to study the unit's "sand tables," scaled mockups of the terrain in Normandy.

By the first of June, the 501st had been marshaled into the airfields from which they would take flight. While the Allied ships stormed the beaches of Normandy, Jim and his fellow paratroops would jump into the Axis-held territory farther inland. "There were 490 planes in the 101st Airborne, with over 6,600 paratroopers. The standard plane was the C-47, the military version of the DC-3." As Jim Carroll described it: "It was the workhorse of the Army." During this first wave of the invasion, every paratrooper would be carrying nearly 100 pounds of equipment.

During their final preparations on the evening of June 5, he noticed some commotion from the other side of the airfield. As it turned out, General Eisenhower had come to meet with several of the paratroopers, wishing them well as they embarked upon the "Great Crusade." The resulting photograph from that meeting became one of the most iconic images of World War II. Jim could see and hear the bustle of activity, but he couldn't get close enough to see Eisenhower. "We wanted to go over and see what was happening but, of course, we couldn't leave our areas."

Nearly an hour after sunset, the first wave of aircraft carrying the 501st departed the British airfield. "England was on double daylight savings time," he recalled, "so it was still light after 10 o' clock at night." Each plane departed the runway at 7-second intervals. "The planes circled for a while as they got into the correct formation…and then headed off over the English Channel." There was still some lingering daylight in the sky as the planes reached their cruising altitude; and Jim recalled seeing faint traces of the invasion fleet below. By his estimate, there must have been thousands of ships headed to the coast of Northern France.

Suddenly, an eruption of anti-aircraft fire shattered the silence of their

Jim Carroll. Paratrooper in the 101st Airborne Division.

predawn flight. As soon as the C-47s vectored over the coast of Normandy: "That's when the fireworks started. Now and then, you could hear a piece of shrapnel hit the side of the airplane." Ironically, Jim admitted that he was too physically ill to be nervous. Motion sickness had once again rendered his stomach unreliable. "There was a slop bucket on the plane for those who had to throw up, but a couple of the guys didn't make it to the bucket. That stench didn't help. Plus, you were carrying all that equipment and you had your parachute harness on as tight as you could get it. I was so miserable; I just didn't care what happened."

Normally, the C-47s would slow down as they approached the drop zone. And Jim could deduce the change in speed by the sound of the planes' engines. "But out plane never slowed down at all," he said. Given the intensity of the *ack-ack* fire, he could hardly blame the pilots for maintaining their top speed.

Slower planes, after all, made easier targets.

"The men formed a line in the middle of the plane and attached their cables to the static line above their heads. It was up to the man behind you to make sure your cable wasn't tangled in your gear." Every paratrooper on board kept his eye on the glowing red light above the fuselage door. Once it turned green, every soldier would jump through the hatch, one after another. Jim recalled the very moment at which the indicator light switched from red to green: "Once the line starts moving, that's it. It's just pushing, pushing, pushing." Within seconds, Jim and his fellow jumpers were out the door.

Seconds later, Jim felt the violent jolt of his canopy opening. And the blast of cold air, as he later recalled, was enough to cure him of his motion sickness. Unlike his training missions in the States, this combat jump was executed from a mere *500 feet*—"and the first hundred feet were spent hoping your parachute was going to open." Of course, Jim's parachute did open, and he landed on the drop zone unscathed.

"The first thing you do is get out of your parachute, and then you have to put your gun together." They had to field strip their rifles for the jump, and had practiced putting them back together in the dark. "I had just got mine together," said Jim, "when I could see these dark forms coming at me."

But these dark forms didn't quite look human.

Not wanting to take a chance, Jim Carroll drew his rifle and pointed it in their direction. Prior to the invasion, every paratrooper had been issued a clicker—"so we could find each other in the dark." One click would be answered by two clicks, thus indicating a fellow trooper. Jim used his clicker, but got no response. The slow-moving forms continued in his direction. His finger was pressed against the trigger when the shapes finally came to light. "Then all at once I could see them. Oh my gosh, they were cows! With all the shells exploding and the airplanes roaring… they were scared and wandering in the field."

Shaking off the bovine encounter, Jim checked his gear and himself. "I wanted to see if I was all in one piece," he said. Luckily, his gear had survived the jump…and he had no visible wounds. "I could barely see a little patch of woods over in the distance, and I headed for that. I felt like I was all alone. I couldn't see even one other trooper around me." But as Jim crept farther into the woods, he began to hear muffled sounds. Not sure if they were humans or more cows, he pulled out his clicker and clicked it. "The response was immediate"—a dozen other clickers rang out in the night.

He had found his comrades.

Unfortunately, these comrades were from a different company. During the chaos of the Normandy invasion, the Allied airborne troops had been scattered across northern France, many of them landing miles away from their intended drop zones. "I didn't know where the rest of my guys were," said Jim, "so I stayed with this group." Together, they marched for nearly a mile to the regiment's objective, "which was to set up a roadblock near Carentan."

Their mission was to block the roads and bridges to prevent the Germans from reinforcing the beaches at Normandy. "It was an interesting four days," he recalled. "We didn't have to worry so much about what was ahead of us…our real problem was with the Germans that were retreating from the beaches. There were firefights all the time." At the end of those four days, however, the airborne troops were relieved by the US infantry units that had broken out from Omaha Beach. "Were we ever glad to see them," he recalled. "They had fresh water and they had food."

After being relieved by the straight-leg infantry, Jim and his fellow paratroopers were sent back to Cherbourg, mopping up pockets of German resistance and wrangling POWs. Then it was back to England for refitting, and a follow-on combat jump into Holland. Like many in the 101st, Jim later found himself in Bastogne for the Battle of the Bulge. When the Third Army finally reached the beleaguered paratroopers, Jim had a fortuitous reunion with his younger brother, Jackson, who was currently serving under Patton's command. In many cases, the war had drawn entire families into its service. Indeed, it wasn't uncommon for every brother within a single family to be drafted into the military. Running into a sibling overseas was always a welcome break from the deadly routines of wartime service.

In all, Jim Carroll made eleven combat jumps with the 101st Airborne Division. When Germany surrendered in May 1945, Jim was alerted that his unit would redeploy to the Pacific. But while training for the possibility of island-hopping combat (and an invasion of the Japanese homeland), Jim was relieved to hear that Japan had surrendered.

After the war, Jim returned to Minnesota and settled into a quiet life as a machinist. For more than twenty years, he was the shop foreman for Durkee-Atwood, a prominent manufacturer of industrial V-belts and other automotive products. Upon his retirement, however, he transitioned into a *second* career as a school bus driver and charter bus driver—jobs he held until the early 2000s.

For most of his adult life, Jim never spoke of the war. However, one day in 1980 when he was ice fishing with his daughter, she asked him why he never shared any of his wartime experiences.

"No one ever asked," he replied.

But in the years that followed, more people began to ask about his experiences in Normandy. This, in turn, led to a number of speaking engagements. These included appearances at schools, community functions, in documentary films, and TV/Radio interviews. In 2014, Senator Amy Klobuchar and the French Council awarded Jim Carroll the French Legion of Honor, recognizing his service in the liberation of France from Nazi occupation.

Jim Carroll passed away on March 28, 2017 at the age of 93.

7
BATTLEGROUND: CBI

DENZEL ALEXANDER (US ARMY) AND BOB MAYNARD (US ARMY, OSS)
IN THE CHINA-BURMA-INDIA THEATER

The China-Burma-India (CBI) theater was, in many ways, the forgotten battlefront of World War II. "There are no infantry divisions here," said one soldier, "only detachments, special units, makeshift outfits, and made-over GIs. All the big divisions are in Europe or on Pacific islands. This is the forgotten war. This is where you fight and die, and nobody seems to give a damn whether your corpse is picked up for a halfway decent burial."

By most accounts, Burma was the epicenter of this human misery. "One day is just like all the others. You climb over vines and see things slither out of the way before you put your foot down. You walk around the thick things that hang from branches because you think you see them move." Indeed, every vine seemed to resemble a snake.

The worst offenders, however, were the leeches.

"They cling to your pants and leggings and squirm to get inside at your blood," said one GI. "Every few minutes you stop and scrape or burn the lousy parasites off your skin. Sometimes, you have to cut them off with a knife because their heads are buried under flesh…sucking your blood. You dig for their heads. If you don't get them out, you'll have a lump the size of a plum. So, you get them, even if it means taking some meat with it."

These sentiments would be echoed by the young Private Denzel Alexander when he arrived in Burma as a combat engineer. Born in Kentucky in 1924, he moved to Detroit when his father became a layout engineer in the automotive industry. On December 7, 1941, Denzel was listening to the afternoon radio when the announcer broke in, saying: "We interrupt this program to announce that Pearl Harbor has been attacked by a large Japanese force." There was no indication of how many had been killed, or what the extent of the damage had been.

But he knew the country was going to war.

"I was almost 18," he said. "I knew I was going to be graduating in a few months and perhaps be drafted."

Initially, Denzel wanted to join the US Army Air Forces. He had been attracted to the pilot lifestyle and, given the manpower needs of the war, the pathways to becoming a pilot had been greatly simplified. "I went to the Air Force induction center to enlist; they gave me an all-day exam"—consisting of a written portion and a physical evaluation. "I passed the written test, and I passed the physicals…but I was five pounds *under*weight."

To his surprise, the Air Force had rejected him for being too skinny.

"And I thought a pilot had to be lightweight!" he chuckled.

"So, a few months later, I was drafted into the Army and put into the Engineer Corps." But while completing his Basic Training at Camp McCoy, Wisconsin (now Fort McCoy), Denzel had one last opportunity to become a pilot. An announcement appeared on the bulletin board, stating that the Air Force needed more pilots to support the upcoming invasions of Italy and France. "They said if you're already in the service, we'll count you as being physically fit," Denzel recalled. "So, if you can pass the written exam, we'll transfer you to the Air Force cadets."

Denzel took the written exam and passed it, again.

"They sent me down to Miami Beach with the cadets and booked me into the New Yorker Hotel." From there, Denzel and his fellow air cadets began pre-flight training, until the cruel mistress of fate (and the Army's bureaucratic myopia) foiled his plans yet again. While he was attending the USAAF ground school, the invasion of Europe was already underway. The Allies had secured a foothold on the Italian mainland and were preparing to descend upon Occupied France. Thus, as Denzel recalled, the Air Force essentially told him: "The invasion has gone so much better and so much faster than we had expected. We've taken in way too many [soldiers] from the regular force [for pilot training]. So, if we took you from the Army after such-and-such date, you will be returned to your unit."

Denzel missed that cutoff date by one week.

"So, there was the *second* time I missed the Air Force!"

The Army then sent him to Fort Bragg, North Carolina, where he was assigned to the 1304th Engineers—"and I went to Burma with that outfit."

Denzel Alexander.

At first, however, he had no idea where the 1304th was going. Europe seemed like the logical destination, given the trajectory of the Allied campaign and the "Europe First" Policy. But as their troop ship, the USS *Anderson*, left Newport News, Virginia, Denzel and his shipmates were surprised to see her steer through the Panama Canal, down to Australia, and up to Bombay, India. And the *Anderson* had made her journey alone. "We weren't part of a convoy," he said, "and the *Anderson* was sleek and fast; we could outrun any submarine."

The 1304th Engineers unloaded at Bombay and boarded a train

eastbound to Burma. "If you ever went across India by train, it was terrible," he said. "You see, India at that time was under British rule. And there were three big sections of India, each controlled by a Maharaja, kind of like a dictator." Each of the three Maharajas had used a different railroad company to lay track within his respective part of the country.

Thus, all three Maharajas had railroads, but the tracks were incongruent to each other.

"They were all different gauges!" Denzel laughed.

So, at various parts of the journey, the 1304th Engineer Battalion had to be ferried across the river by rowboat, two men at a time. At that capacity, it took an entire day for the battalion to cross the river. "It was really something," he said, "I wouldn't want to do it again. But we got into Burma, and we were there to build the Ledo Road"—later known as the famous "Stillwell Road."

"Burma was a lot like Florida," Denzel recalled—"a long and narrow nation. The old Burma Road ran all the way up Burma into the Himalaya Mountains and over into China. Well, the Japs had conquered Burma. And for us to try to come up *through* Burma, well, that would have taken us a long time and a lot of expenses. So, we came from the north, through the jungles of Burma and built the Ledo Road to hook up with the old Burma Road."

Specifically, Denzel's unit had been tasked to build tactical bridges along the road. "We built three kinds: wooden bridges for smaller streams; pontoon bridges for medium-sized streams; and Bailey bridges for large rivers. We built those all across Burma. The jungle had a lot of streams flowing down out of the mountains, and there had to be a bridge there, otherwise you couldn't get trucks and tanks through it."

But the bridge-building operations were fraught with peril... particularly from the prying eyes of the Japanese. "Merrill's Marauders had driven all the Japanese out of North Burma," he said, "but they would come up the river at night." Denzel knew that the Japanese still had spies in the area; and if a bridge were about to be finished, "they would come up the river at night and try to blow it up." As Denzel recalled: "We had machine guns set up on both sides of the river and hidden in the jungle"—ready to open fire at the first sign of enemy movement.

Thankfully, the Japanese never reached any of Denzel's bridges.

"And we did sink an awful lot of their boats!"

At times, however, it seemed that Denzel had more to fear from the local wildlife than the Japanese. "A lot of things happened in the jungle," he said. "The jungle is not like a forest. A forest has trees; the jungle has *everything*. And at certain times between building a bridge, we'd have some free time and we could pretty much do what we wanted. So, three of us decided to go out and explore the jungle."

Denzel and his two friends hit the trails until they came upon a fallen tree.

One of his more daring comrades jumped atop the fallen trunk, using the low-lying branches to hoist himself up. His climbing expedition was cut short, however, when he came face-to-face with a cobra.

"And this one was *big!*" Denzel recalled.

By his recollection, its body was as thick as a human arm. "It was leaning over the tree, spitting at us." Denzel's buddy fell from the tree in a panic, but Denzel quickly shot the snake with his M1 rifle. "We decided not to go any farther."

A few days later, while sleeping in his tent, Denzel awoke feeling an odd sensation on his chest. Each tent could hold three soldiers, sleeping on their standard-issue Army cots. "I woke up sometime in the middle of the night...the moon isn't shining and its cloudy, pitch black. I couldn't see a thing, but I kept feeling something on my chest." From what he could deduce, this foreign object had a long, thin body with a wider mass at its top.

"I was convinced it was a cobra."

Snakes were cold-blooded, and often slipped into warmer areas to maintain their body heat. This cobra had likely crawled through the tent flap and slithered into his cot.

"What in the world am I going to do?" he thought to himself.

"My first thought was, well, just stay here all night," and perhaps the snake would slither away on its own. But then he realized if he fell asleep, and inadvertently shifted his body, the snake would bite him. "To be bit by a cobra in the jungle...forget it! I figured the snake was over my left arm, but my right arm was free." Thus, Denzel reasoned that he could grab the cobra by its hood with his right hand, lift it up, and grab its lower body with his left hand, incapacitating the snake long enough for his friends to kill it with their bayonets.

Silently, Denzel began to psych himself up.

"Ok, on the count of three...1, 2, 3...I couldn't do it. Second time: 1, 2, 3...I *still* couldn't do it." He kept thinking the snake would bite him in the neck.

"Finally, I said I've got to do it. So...1, 2, 3...and I grabbed it!"

As Denzel screamed and strangled the offensive snake, he realized that this "snake" was, in fact, his own left arm. His left arm had fallen asleep and he hadn't even realized it. Still, the commotion had been enough to awaken his tentmates, both of whom scrambled for their flashlights.

"Denzel! What's the matter?!"

But Denzel, now realizing he was ahold of his left arm, wasn't going to admit that he had mistaken his own appendage for a venomous snake. "If I tell them," he thought, "I'll be known as the 'snake man' for the rest of my time here." He thus turned to his tentmates and said: "Sorry, I guess I just had a bad dream. Go on back to sleep."

Imaginary reptiles notwithstanding, Denzel's most memorable story from his time in Burma involved a seemingly ill-fated cargo pilot trying to navigate the "Hump" of the Himalayas. "The Himalayas are the highest mountains in the world; and the Burma Road weaved around through the Himalaya Mountains into China." But until the Allies could retake those sections of the Burma Road, the only way to get supplies into China was by air. "And we called it 'flying over the 'Hump.'" The Allied cargo planes, however, were often so heavily-laden that they couldn't gain enough altitude to fly over the Himalayan peaks. They had to fly at lower altitudes between and amongst the mountainsides and jagged escarpments. As expected, maneuvering a utility plane among these imposing obstacles required a high degree of airmanship.

"We had one pilot," said Denzel, "who had some heavy equipment and had to take two or three extra men to come along and show the Chinese how to operate it." The pilot, his crew, and the additional tag-alongs took off from Burma and went flying through the mountains. But as he rounded the plane between two peaks, he suddenly realized he had made a wrong turn.

"He was in a box canyon," Denzel recalled.

This problematic piece of terrain had steep walls on three sides, and only *one* point of egress...which was now behind them. "He couldn't park anywhere, and he couldn't turn around," Denzel continued. "So, he started trying to climb over that [canyon wall] at the end." The not-so-nimble cargo plane began climbing so steeply, rattling and trembling, that the pilot was certain his engine would stall.

Miraculously, however, the plane made it over the canyon wall, but not without scraping its underbelly against the jutting rocks. "It tore out the bottom of the fuselage, ripping a hole about six feet wide along the bottom," whereupon the plane started losing altitude. Meanwhile, the errant pilot turned to his crew and said: "Men, we're not going to make it. The only thing we can do is this: If you five men will bail out"—pointing to the five heaviest crewmen aboard—"you can make it back to northern

Bob Maynard.

Burma by tonight." The pilot insisted that he would try to stay airborne with the equipment operators in tow.

"If I can make it [into China], fine. If not, I'll have to bail out, too," said the pilot.

The five heavier airmen reluctantly strapped on their parachutes and did as they were told. "Five heavy men," said Denzel, "could weigh close to half a ton," thus reducing the plane's overall weight, and giving the pilot a chance to land at his destination in China.

The five parachuting airmen made it back to the Allied airfield, "but we never heard whether the pilot had made it," said Denzel. "We kept asking, and every time we'd see an airman, we'd ask: 'Did you hear about that pilot?'" Yet nobody seemed to know what had happened to the pilot or his plane. "There were three or four landing bases on the other side of the mountain," Denzel recalled. So, there were no guarantees of finding an airman with knowledge of the seemingly-doomed cargo plane.

Yet, several years later, a chance encounter with a VA doctor in Florida revealed the fate of that wayward pilot. After the war, Denzel was ordained as a Baptist minister and pastored a church in Palm Bay, Florida for several years. Before his final relocation to Minnesota, Denzel was chatting with his young VA doctor:

"Hey Denzel," said the young doctor, "I never did ask you; where did you serve?"

"Burma…near the Himalayas."

"Oh, my father was over there."

"Oh?" said Denzel. "Was he working on the road?"

"No, he was in the Air Force; but let me tell you an interesting story."

The young doctor proceeded to tell him the story about how his father had been flying a plane (carrying a load of heavy equipment) whose bottom was torn off by a canyon cliff, which in turn precipitated an early bailout for the five heaviest crewmen on board.

"You gotta be kidding me!!" Denzel exclaimed. "I've been trying to get the answer to that for years. Did he make it?"

"Oh yea, he made it," the doctor beamed. "He's here in Florida with me and my mother…they live about two doors down."

After several decades of preaching, Denzel Alexander retired from the pulpit in the early 2000s. Now at the age of 97, he lives quietly with his family in Chanhassen, Minnesota.

On December 7, 1941, Bob Maynard was an Ivy League student, enjoying his life as a college baseball player at Princeton University. In 1943, however, he left the comforts of academia and joined the US Army at Fort Bragg, North Carolina. Having some college under his belt, he applied for and was accepted to Officer Candidate School (OCS) at Fort Sill, Oklahoma. Commissioned as a Field Artillery officer in May 1944, he was made a forward observer (FO).

The FO, as he described it, was a liaison of death.

He could ensure delivery of deadly-accurate cannon fire. "But, if you make a mistake in your mathematical calculations, you can bring fire down on yourself."

As a newly-minted artilleryman, he arrived at Fort Jackson, South Carolina—one of the primary hubs for personnel going to the European Theater. However, he had barely set foot on Fort Jackson when he was cornered by a Major Weiner, who was compiling a list of the top-rated artillery officers coming through the stateside Replacement Depot. "He asked me a series of questions," Bob recalled.

"Do you have any college?"

"Any foreign language experiences?"

"Do you have any objections to taking parachute training?"

"Do you have any dependents?"

Bob grew more uncomfortable with each passing question…until Weiner asked him: "Would you prefer being in an outfit where you have some degree of discretion over your own destiny, and plan innovative things on your missions?"

Weiner was recruiting for the Office of Strategic Services (OSS).

Bob liked the idea of having autonomy…and being in a unit where creativity was rewarded rather than punished. One week later, he received orders to Washington, DC.

"The people at Jackson thought it was a very strange order," he said, "because you normally got orders to go from base to base," and almost never to DC. His orders included a message to call a Washington-based telephone number. "I called it and they told me that the next morning, I would be taken in for psychological training."

It was perhaps the most peculiar experience of his young life.

For psychological training, each of the OSS candidates were hoarded into the same building and, regardless of rank, were dressed in unmarked Army fatigues. "You didn't know if the guy next to you was an Admiral, or a private, or a sergeant…and we all had false names and backgrounds." Indeed, each of the candidates had been given a character role, and was told to keep that identity while mingling with his comrades. As Bob recalled: "I was supposed to be from Kansas, and my dad was supposed to be a college professor out there." In reality, Bob was from New Jersey, and his father had *no* ties to academia. Throughout this role-playing exercise, "psychiatrists would observe if you were a good leader or a good follower," said Bob, "because you don't need all leaders, you need some followers."

Five days later, Bob and the other candidates progressed to the physical evaluation trials. To his surprise, this portion of the training took place in a "great big mansion," he said, "without much furniture." Apart from the OSS trainees, Bob noticed that many of the mansion's residents were GIs who had been wounded in combat. Unbeknownst to Bob, however, this "mansion" was the former Congressional Country Club. "It had gone bankrupt, and General [Bill] Donovan had rented it as a rest home for people coming back from overseas duty, and for those training to go overseas." The physical portion of the OSS training included a lot of "creeping and crawling under barbed wire, jumping off practice towers for parachute training, and explosives going off all over the place." Curiously, the man in charge of the physical regimen was Wes Fesler—a college football Hall of Famer who later became head coach for the University of Minnesota.

Upon completing the physical module of his OSS pre-selection, Bob reported to OSS Headquarters, near the Old Naval Hospital in Washington, DC. He was one of five OSS selectees reporting to Headquarters that day—"and the man in charge said we were very lucky because '109' was in town, and he wanted to talk to new arrivals."

Bob had no idea who this "109" may have been; but he sounded important.

"So, we all went over to the next building…and there was '109'— it was Major General Bill Donovan." Known as "Wild Bill," General Donovan was already a legend within the American defense community. He had been awarded the Medal of Honor, the Distinguished Service Cross, *and* the Croix de Guerre for his service in World War I. He had also been an Assistant Attorney General under Calvin Coolidge. His colorful personality (and candid bluntness), however, didn't always sit well with the Washington establishment. "He was an expert at stepping on toes," said Bob, "and people said he had as many enemies in Washington as he did overseas."

Today, Donovan wasted no time. When he met the young Bob Maynard, he asked him: "Lieutenant, do you know why you're here?"

"No sir," Bob replied.

"Well, I don't either," said Donovan. "But we'll find something interesting and worthwhile for you to do."

Bob later said that this exchange was illustrative of how the OSS recruited its personnel. In the military, established units were sent on missions according to their function—for example, a fighter squadron or an armored division. In the OSS, however, units were formed *ad hoc* from a "pool" of specialists. "We had doctors, radio operators, demolition experts, map readers, and even people we'd gotten out of Alcatraz who were good forgers…because we had to forge a lot of documents in the work we were doing."

At first, the OSS had tapped Bob for duty in the Philippines, where he'd be spying on enemy ship movements. But it soon came to light that any OSS operatives within General MacArthur's territory would be transferred directly to his command.

"And that was unacceptable to Bill Donovan," said Bob.

In fact, Donovan and MacArthur had been professional rivals and "frenemies" since serving together under General John Pershing during the hunt for Pancho Villa. As a result of this bureaucratic rivalry between the OSS and MacArthur's Southwest Pacific Area command, Bob Maynard soon found himself reassigned to the CBI theater.

"I was put on the slow boat to China, down around Australia, and into Calcutta," he said, where he boarded the train to the Chabua Airfield in India. It was the primary hub for flights going "over the hump" of the Himalayas to deliver supplies into China. By now, Stillwell's men had driven the Japanese back to the Burma Road, but the enemy's air defense capabilities over the Himalayas were still going strong. "They shot down an awful lot of C-47s and their escorts," Bob recalled. "And if the Japs didn't get them, the air currents and bad weather got a lot more. That passageway through the Himalayas was called 'The Aluminum Graveyard,'"—but Bob's flight over the hump was surprisingly pleasant. "We didn't have any attacks, and we landed in Kunming."

Reporting to OSS Detachment 202, Bob met Colonel Richard Heppner, the officer-in-charge. Heppner said that he had looked through the records of his incoming personnel, and found a job that might suit Bob well. "It was coordinating missions," said Bob—ensuring that the field agents got what they needed, and that their intelligence data was passed along to the right venue.

"It was, I think, the best job in the OSS for the CBI theater," said Bob.

As a rule of thumb, everything in the OSS was on a "need-to-know" basis. No information was shared among the different operational sections unless it facilitated their unique missions. For example, an agent in the OSS Propaganda Section didn't know what the Sabotage Section was doing, or what the Air Operations Section was doing. "They were all separate," Bob remembered.

Coordinating spy missions was a monumental job for a young lieutenant, and Bob was certain that there were more-qualified individuals than he. "But I had three qualifications that no one else had," he recalled. "First, I was available…most of the people who arrived [in Det 202] already had assignments. Second, they noticed I came out of the Field Artillery,"—Colonel Heppner and his executive officer, Major Bill Davis, were both artillerymen. "But the clincher was that Heppner, Davis, and I had all played baseball at Princeton. That's what did it!" he laughed.

Taking stock of his new responsibilities as an intelligence coordinator, Bob had his work cut out for him. "China was chaotic," he remembered. "There were espionages on all sides…even amongst the Allies!" As Bob recalled, Chiang Kai-shek, Mao Zedong, the British, and the French were all spying on each other. To make matters worse, Chiang and Mao seemed to be more interested in killing each other than fighting the Japanese. From what Bob could deduce, the collective attitude between Mao's Communists and the Kuomintang was: "Let the Westerners defeat the Japanese. In the meantime, we're going to hoard things so we can fight each other and gain control of China after the war."

In April 1945, a few months into his duties as an intelligence coordinator, Bob received an unexpected visit from Wild Bill Donovan, the commanding general whom he'd met in Washington prior to arriving at Detachment 202.

"He came to China for a surprise visit," said Bob, "and he didn't bring an aide."

However, remembering Bob from their prior meeting at OSS Headquarters, Donovan tapped him to be his aide. "I got to know him and had some amusing but meaningful experiences with him."

One such experience included Donovan's need for a barber. On his first day at the OSS station, Donovan asked:

"Do we have a barber here, Lieutenant?"

"Yes sir. We can have him here in the morning."

"Good, because I need a haircut and a shave."

Detachment 202 had a young corporal who provided haircuts as a hobbyist barber. But when Bob approached him with a request to cut General Donovan's hair, the corporal refused. "I couldn't cut his hair; I'd be too nervous."

But luckily, Bob had a contingency plan.

As it turned out, the OSS staff also got their haircuts from a local Chinese man—"tall, about 60 years old, with a smock and a scraggly beard." The Chinese barber arrived as requested, and sat down in front of Donovan, opening his pigskin satchel to reveal a full complement of barber tools—including scissors and a straight razor.

"Is this one of our men?" asked Donovan.

"Well," said Bob, "he cuts our hair, sir."

"Has he been cleared for security?"

Bob Maynard (left) stands with Major General William Donovan and the members of OSS Detachment 202.

"I don't think so," Bob winced.

"And you're going to let him near my neck with *those*?" Donovan asked, pointing to the scissors and razor. Indeed, no one in Detachment 202 had vetted this Chinese barber to ensure he had no enemy connections. Luckily, the young corporal was standing by, and quickly jumped in to give Donovan a fresh haircut and a smooth shave.

All the while, Bob sat nervously, expecting that once the haircut was complete, he'd get a severe reprimand, or possibly terminated from the OSS. But to his surprise (and his relief) Donovan simply stood up from his chair and said: "The corporal would have been a better first choice, don't you think so, Lieutenant?"

Bob nodded in agreement.

But such was the way Donovan handled his subordinates. Simple redirections got better results than terse reprimands.

The next morning, Donovan was inspecting the grounds of the OSS station when he asked Bob how the staff maintained physical security of the compound. "Well, the compound has walls around it," said Bob, "we have an Officer of the Day, with guards, and we have Doberman Pinchers" on roving patrols.

"Well," said Donovan, "I'm holding *you* personally responsible."

Donovan was only kidding, but the young Bob Maynard thought he was serious. Still, Bob took Donovan's playful admonition to a curious extreme. Indeed, the next morning, Donovan found Colonel Heppner.

"You know what this kid did last night?" he told Heppner, referring to Bob.

"I was kidding when I told him about the security," Donovan continued. "But I tried to get out of my room last night to use the bathroom and I couldn't get out…he had moved his bed against the door!" Apparently, Bob had barricaded Donovan's door in case the high walls, roving guards, and Doberman Pinchers failed to stop an advancing intruder. But by the same token, Bob hadn't realized that the impromptu barricade would have also prevented Donovan's easy egress from the room.

Donovan and Heppner just laughed.

Donovan's trip to China had three objectives, all of which were top secret. "He knew about the Atomic Bomb, the timing, and what the plans were," Bob remembered. As such, Donovan's first order of business was to meet with Allied commanders in the CBI and ask them: "If this war ended soon, who do you anticipate taking over from the Japanese in Burma, Laos, and China?" Although Donovan had posed the question as a hypothetical, Bob said Donovan already knew the answer: Given the trajectory of this conflict, there was no way the European powers could hold onto their colonial possessions much longer. Nationalist forces were already on the rise in India, Burma, and French Indochina.

Second, Donovan had to compile data for President Roosevelt, outlining permanent functions for the OSS after the war. "But FDR died and Truman put it on the backburner," said Bob. Still, Donovan's memos outlined the doctrinal precepts for what would become the modern CIA…including espionage and propaganda. "There were two kinds of propaganda," Bob continued, "*white* propaganda, which was just the news; and *black* propaganda, where you make things up that are to your benefit, lies included. That's what our OSS propaganda section did." Part and parcel to Donovan's theories was to collectivize intel data into a "central intelligence" apparatus that could easily relay information to different field agencies. "Prior to that," said Bob, "the Army had its own intelligence staff; the Navy had its own staff; the FBI had theirs"—and these agencies rarely spoke to one another.

Third, Donovan had come to China to organize teams to rescue Allied POWs in Manchuria and elsewhere throughout the CBI because, as Bob recalled: "Intelligence showed that the Japanese pattern was to either execute POWs at the end of the war, abandon them, or put them on another Death March."

However, Donovan nearly lost *all* the paperwork for these top-secret missions when the Kunming OSS station flooded. During a torrential downpour, the rising water (polluted by raw sewage and street litter) had seeped into the compound, thereby forcing Donovan and his staff to eat their meals at a local Chinese restaurant until the flood receded.

Naturally, Donovan wouldn't leave his briefcase containing his top-secret documents behind at the compound. After all, it contained critical data about the rescue of prisoners and details about the Atomic Bomb. "It was too secure to leave back at Headquarters, so he carried it himself into the restaurant."

After lunch, though, as Donovan, Heppner, and Bob Maynard got back into the car, Donovan turned to Heppner and said:

"Dick, do you have the briefcase?"

"No sir," he replied.

"Lieutenant, do you have it?"

"No sir."

It was then that they realized Donovan had left his briefcase under the restaurant table. "And none of us had the guts to tell him 'Sir, you had it.'" Bob recalled with a chuckle. "And so, we drove back and I ran into the restaurant," said Bob, who was relieved to see that, even among the lunchtime crowd, the briefcase was still under the table.

Bob quickly retrieved it and darted back into the car.

After a brief period of silence, Donovan broke the tension, saying: "I won't tell anyone if you won't." All three of them laughed.

Bob's tour as Donovan's aide also put him in contact with another OSS agent, Paul Cushing Child, "who was in charge of the secret war room, where they had a map and they moved pins," said Bob. "All he did, all day, was move pins wherever we had agents and operations going on," allowing Donovan and the station chiefs to have real-time situational awareness of where the OSS teams were operating within the CBI.

Bob soon discovered that Paul had a girlfriend: another OSS operative, Julia McWilliams.

Standing at 6'2," she was decidedly tall for a woman. So tall, in fact, that she had been rejected by the WACs and the WAVES. Casting her lot with the OSS, McWilliams eventually arrived at the Kunming station alongside Bob Maynard, where she catalogued the high volume of classified data coming in from field agents. As Bob recalled, if an OSS team needed to blow up a bridge on the Yellow River, "they would go to Julia, and she'd know how many Japanese were nearby; what the bridge construction was; what its weak points were; and how many aircraft might be available." After the war, McWilliams married Paul Child, taking his surname and becoming "Julia Child," the famous chef and American TV personality.

After the war, Bob returned to Princeton, graduating with a degree in international relations. He elected to stay in the Army Reserve, and simultaneously earned a law degree from Harvard. With the outbreak of the Korean War in 1950, Bob was recalled from the Army Reserve and placed in the Counterintelligence Corps. After his final release from the Army in 1953, Bob worked as a corporate attorney: first for the United Shoe Machinery Corporation in Boston; then for Honeywell in Minneapolis. He retired in 1985 as the Senior VP of Legal Affairs for Honeywell. He continued to reside in the Minneapolis–St. Paul area until his passing in 2017, at the age of 94.

8

FROGMAN

DAVID GOULD,
NAVY COMBAT DIVER

Climbing to the edge of the black water, Dave Gould readied himself for the oncoming plunge. The muffled gurgling of the PT boat's engine seemed to egg him on as he waited for the signal... "Gould. Get set! Ready, now! Go!"

Dropping over the side, and into the balmy waters of the South Pacific, he re-surfaced just in time to hear the revving of the PT's engine fade into the distance. Just above the waves, barely visible in the moonlight, was the dim outline of Eniwetok—the menacing atoll that had just become the latest target in the "island hopping" campaign.

Swimming towards the amorphous land mass, Dave took stock of the items strapped to his body—Colt .45, a graph paper mapping board... and his cyanide capsule. The training manual had made this poisonous pill sound so matter-of-fact: "If about to be captured, break the capsule in your teeth. Death will be quick and painless"—a fair alternative to what the Japanese would do to him.

Dave Gould was a combat diver—a "Frogman"—but not by choice. In fact, he had become a frogman in the most old-fashioned way: Instead of volunteering, he had been volun-*told*. When he enlisted in the Navy, he had requested to become a Seabee—the Navy's combat engineers. The term "Seabee" came from the abbreviation "CB," referring to the Navy's construction battalions. This rating seemed like a good fit, considering he had been a metalworker before the war. But a seemingly-innocent disclosure on his Classification Card had roped him into the world of combat diving. Under the heading labeled "Hobbies," he wrote "Swimming." After all, he had grown up on the beaches of Long Island, where swimming was a way of life.

Having been tapped for dive training, the Navy quickly hastened him to Underwater Demolitions (UD) school in California. UD was an integral part of the Frogman's repertoire. If he wasn't laying sea mines, he was diffusing them. He was expected to be, in equal parts, a demolitions expert *and* a reconnaissance specialist—taking note of the enemy dispositions, capabilities, and strongpoints. Frogmen like him were part of an elite subculture—the burgeoning "special operations" community. These Frogmen would become the forefathers of the modern-day Navy SEALs.

Tonight was January 6, 1944, his first plunge into the waters surrounding Eniwetok. "It would be six weeks yet before the vast invasion force hit the beaches here," he recalled.

And tonight, Dave wasn't alone.

Elsewhere along the atoll, other Frogmen were treading through the perilous waters, preparing to clear the way for the Allied ground troops that would storm the beaches. This would be the first of four visits Dave Gould would make to the remote atoll. He would come again ten days before the invasion. Then, a third visit the night before D-Day. "And then, hit the beach with the assault wave on D-Day itself"—guiding a platoon of Marine infantry to key points along the enemy's redoubts.

On this first night at Eniwetok, however, he stopped about 100 yards offshore, treading water as he studied the Japanese fortifications in the moonlight. "If there were sentries or guard posts," he said, "they were well-concealed." Swimming over to the edge of the reef, he realized that the landing craft could easily ride over it during high tides. Trafficability of the reef as a function of tides was a critical detail for mission planning— "a matter of life and death," he said, for the Marines and soldiers who would soon be storming the beach.

Wading into the shallows, Dave pulled the mapping board from his leg. Extracting a small grease pencil from his sheath, he began to annotate the enemy fortifications on his map. Under a nearby palm grove stood the telltale figure of a pillbox. "There, off to the right a bit," he said, "a roundish mound indicated a gun pit—a long barrel jutted over it, close to the ground. Nearby were other emplacements, probably for machine guns to sweep the beach." All told, he was confident that the pre-invasion bombardment would make short work of these defenses.

As he waded back and forth across the beach, he was careful to avoid the ominous sea mines bobbing in the water—"ready to set off a blast on contact." But these mines weren't the only obstacles awaiting the Allied landing force. "Metal boat traps loomed silently under the shallows. Trip wires etched faint lines along the sand."

Suddenly, a crouching noise rang out from the beach.

Ducking down into the shallows, Dave saw the faintly luminous silhouette of two Japanese sentries walking along the shore. They were so close that Dave could hear them talking, even over the sound of the breaking waves.

"That had been close!" A little too close for comfort.

In fact, these close calls reminded him how ironically fortunate he was to have the cyanide capsule. If the Japanese captured him, they would gleefully torture and kill him—but not before extracting as much information as possible.

His watch now read 3:00am. "Time to start back." A Frogman had only *one* chance to rendezvous with his pickup boat. For if he missed the incoming PT boat, it wouldn't risk another pass to look for him in the darkness. "That might tip off the whole invasion approach," he said. Thus, if a Frogman missed his boat, he had two options: (1) swim out to sea, hoping to find a friendly base before the sharks got to him, or (2) swim ashore and evade the enemy by living in the bush. "That was damn unlikely on a small island like Eniwetok," he said. "No place to hide!"

It was nearly dawn when Dave reached the pickup point, one mile out from the beach. In the pre-dawn darkness, he could see the heads of his fellow Frogmen, bobbing along the water as they waited for the pickup boat. Suddenly, the PT boat appeared over the horizon, piercing the charcoal-gray aura of the morning darkness with its rambling Packard engine. As the boat came nearer, Dave could see the pickup man seated at the bow.

"A heavy loop was slung around his shoulder," he recalled, "trailed down over the side."

What ensued was a carefully-rehearsed choreography wherein the pickup man would lower the loop down to the surface, ready to catch the extended arm of the nearest frogman, hoisting him aboard.

When the pickup man got to Dave, he caught the loop with such brute force that it felt as though his shoulder might rip off. Tumbling back onto the deck of the PT, Dave thought to himself:

"Visit Number One is nearly over—thank the Lord!"

The PT boat raced out to its destroyer escort. Once aboard, Dave would be debriefed by the shipboard intelligence officers, examining his maps and asking him what he'd seen along the nighttime shores.

Four weeks later, Dave returned to Eniwetok for his second visit. "This was no mere reconnaissance trip," he said.

This time, he was laden with explosives.

"A string of wires, detonators, and sub-surface buoys" trailed behind him as he swam through the night. Tonight, he was putting his demolition skills to the test.

As he swam up the ring of floating mines, he carefully taped blocks of TNT between their deadly spikes, fastening the lead wires with a tailor's dexterity. Nimble, steady hands were a necessity in this line of work. One false move could detonate the sea mine, killing him and alerting the Japanese to other Frogmen's presence. While fastening the TNT to some of the floating mines, Dave successfully disarmed others—slowly but deftly unscrewing the Japanese detonator caps.

For the underwater tank traps, Dave intermittently taped them with alternating quantities of high explosive charges and a dollop of plastic explosives. Either of these demolition assets would suffice to disable the tank traps. Fastening the lead lines and trip lines, he strung them out to the deeper waters beyond the reef, securing each one to a marker buoy. He then dove down, anchoring the buoy, and preparing it for the "electric plunger detonator," that he would attach the night before D-Day.

On the eve of the invasion, he prepped the last of his offshore demolitions before wading back to the atoll. Tonight, he would reconnoiter the inland Japanese outposts *on foot*. The Intelligence staff wanted him to "find lanes of access off the beach and into the island"—presumably without getting captured.

As he quietly ambled onto the beach, his skin crawled as he beheld the sight in front of him. The displaced sand revealed an unmistakable pattern of anti-personnel mines.

The Japanese knew the invasion fleet was on its way.

Moving like a shadow amongst the trees, Dave spied a narrow road leading up from the beach. Several yards inland, the road ended at a cluster of buildings—barracks for the Japanese defenders. "An attack down the road would run right into them," he said, "flat, open areas good for flanking attacks."

From his shadowy redoubts in the jungle, Dave could hear the muffled staccato of enemy voices piercing through the night. "The place was crawling with Japanese." Not wanting to press his luck any further, Dave slowly withdrew towards the beach, back into the surf, and out to his designated pickup point.

"D-Day was tomorrow morning," he said. And the American task force would initiate its pre-dawn bombardment within a few hours.

Marines storm the beaches of Eniwetok as an SBD Dauntless flies overhead.

"Off the shores of Eniwetok, a vast fleet of American warships lay in the darkness. Thundering guns of warships made the night one roaring bedlam. Deep in their dugouts and pillboxes, the Japanese defenders cowered as all hell raged roaring above them."

On the morning of D-Day, Dave Gould stood aboard the transport USS *Middleton*, conferring with the Marine infantrymen whom he'd be guiding along the beach. "Get up the beach and through the narrow strip of woods fast," he said. "Set your machine guns up damn fast. Then you can sweep the road and open space in front of the barracks—what's left of them. That's as far as I can lead you. Beyond that, it's up to you guys."

Climbing down into the landing craft, he crouched down near the helmsman. It was up to Dave to guide this helmsman around the reef and point out significant landmarks along the shore. And for this mission, Dave had traded his normal scuba gear for the full complement of battle regalia—"Helmet, pistol, ammo belt, and full combat kit, ready for the assault." He had no rifle, but his Colt 45 could inflict *some* damage on the enemy. Then, too, it was an unspoken rule that he could pick up any rifle or machine gun from the nearest fallen comrade.

As the landing craft neared the reef, naval gunfire was thundering overhead, pounding into the shore to keep the enemy's head down. Just outside the reef, their landing craft stopped long enough for Dave to jump over the side and fasten his plunger detonator to the pre-set buoy. Treading water while the sea rattled from Allied naval guns, Dave fastened the lead wires and rammed down on the plunger. The beach erupted into a "boiling wall of water, coral fragments, and pieces of flying metal," he said. "It was done, the way was open." His pre-set demolitions had cleared the way for all landing craft in their sector.

Eager Marines happily pulled him back onboard. Checking his personal gear one more time, he signaled to the helmsman:

"Okay. All clear. Come on in!"

The landing craft crunched into the surf just moments after the naval bombardment lifted from the beach. "Flights of planes screamed in, overhead, raking the battered area beyond the beach with bombs and guns." Along the beach, the lush palm trees had been reduced to charred and battered stumps. But from among these destroyed palms and peppered pillboxes, a few surviving Japanese began returning fire. Somehow, they had survived the naval onslaught, and they were determined to make the Americans pay for it. Clouds of sand erupted as bullets and mortars rained down along the beachhead.

"Down ramp!" a voice cried out.

As the mechanical ramp dropped into the surf, Dave and his Marines ran headlong into the fiery beach. "That way—around the side of the pillbox!" he yelled, pointing to the structure he had mapped on his first visit. "The men ran heavily up the beach," he recalled, "and dove to earth in the edge of the shattered tree stumps."

All seemed to be going well...until Dave felt the fiery sensation of a Japanese bullet slamming into his left leg. His entire leg seemed to have been jerked out from underneath him. Feeling the onrush of blood, however, Dave was somewhat relieved to see that his leg was still intact, but a pulsating wound had just emerged from above his knee. Digging for his First Aid pouch, he unsheathed the field dressing for a hasty but effective tourniquet. As he pulled himself up from the sand, he faintly heard a voice shouting:

"Goddamnit! Gould, where the hell are you?!"

In the opening rounds of the melee, his platoon had lost sight of him. Hobbling half-erect up the slope to his immediate front, he told himself:

"You can navigate boy! Get off this damned beach!"

Dave found his Marines as he descended into the tangled mess of fallen trees at the crest of the slope. They were maneuvering their way to the edge of the road, but the Japanese were likewise taking up their own positions, ready to lay down some deadly return fire. Dave hobbled over to the two closest Marines, a machine gunner and his assistant gunner (AG). The two-man machine gun teams were a deadly duo: one man firing while the other fed his ammunition into the gun, changing barrels as needed.

But before they could open fire, the gunner was killed by an enemy bullet.

His shocked AG sat there in a dazed, catatonic stupor until Dave crawled up behind him.

"Snap out of it, Mac!" Dave thundered.

"Keep the belt feeding smooth. They'll be here any second now."

Dave's words were uncannily prophetic. For within moments, another Marine farther down the line yelled: "Here they come!" But Dave was ready. He knew the area well. "Good field of fire, right across the flat."

From across the open field, a hoard of Japanese soldiers came thundering towards the American lines. "An officer led them," Dave recalled, "swinging a glistening samurai sword in circles over his head. They were screaming hysterically as they came."

It was the classic *Banzai* charge.

"Keep that belt feed smooth!" he yelled to the AG.

Dave hammered down on the trigger, sweeping the machine gun from side to side.

He was aghast at how many Nipponese warriors were falling under the fury of his automatic fire—medleys of pink and red mists spouted into the air as innards and brain matter were littering the battlefield. And Dave was even more aghast at how many of them kept charging the line with unflinching fanaticism, unfazed by the blood and carnage erupting all around them.

"A red glow began to show as the barrel became overheated."

But there was no time to change it now—the enemy was closing in fast. The barrel shimmied and rattled as Dave kept the trigger pressed tightly against its well. But just when it seemed the barrel would explode from overheating, the last *Banzai* charger fell from view. "The field was full of twisted, sprawling bodies." Dave grimly wondered how many of them had been killed by his own gun. But he didn't have too long to consider the carnage. For within a few moments of the last gunshot,

Dave's wounded leg finally caught up to him—he passed out from the loss of blood.

He regained consciousness two days later aboard the *Middleton*; he had been patched up by a local corpsman. His leg was stiff, but not broken. Aside from the loss of blood, he was otherwise intact. "Able to fight another day!" the corpsman told him.

And David Gould would fight for many more days…swimming recon missions at Kwajalein, Palau, and Leyte Gulf. After the war, he returned to his native New York and re-entered the metalworking industry, eventually rising to become a Fabrication Superintendent. Like many from the Greatest Generation, Dave Gould often stayed mum about the war, and was unimpressed by his own deeds. "Look," he said, "the war was a dirty job that had to be done. So we did it. I was suited for Frogman combat, so that's why they put me in. That's all." Dave Gould passed away in 1983.

9

IWO JIMA: THE SHADOWS OF SURIBACHI

GILBERTO MENDEZ:
FROM THE MEXICAN ARMY TO THE US MARINE CORPS

G ilberto "Gil" Mendez was the youngest of *seventeen* children (nine boys; eight girls) born to Sebastian and Maria Arroyo Mendez. His parents had fled Mexico during the Revolution of 1910, settling in San Antonio, Texas, where Gil was born. "They were legal residents," he emphasized, "and what they knew best was agriculture." Like many others who had fled from the Revolution, Gil's parents sought refuge across the border in Texas. "So, they settled down, and they worked in seasonal agricultural crops…fruit and vegetables, they were the most abundant crops to be harvested."

Although money was tight, Gil recalled that his family was exceptionally close. The older children were expected to work, while the younger siblings attended school. Growing up on the rural outskirts of San Antonio, Gil recalled that there were "no hospitals, no clinics, no nothing"—thus facilitating the use of natural remedies handed down through generations of Mexican tradition. Gil proudly recalled that each of his siblings were born at home with the assistance of a midwife. No doctors or fancy obstetrics needed.

"Unfortunately, when we came of age," said Gil, "the Depression had already started." This led to a severe backlash against Mexican immigrants living in the American Southwest. Known as the "Mexican Repatriation," the US government deported more than 80,000 Mexicans, many of whom were legal residents like the Mendez family. "I was never able to comprehend how you can expatriate an American citizen,"— Gil and many of his siblings were, after all, American-born. "We were repatriated to Mexico [but] we were not *citizens* of Mexico." Gil claimed Mexican heritage, of course, but not Mexican citizenship. Yet, because his parents were Mexican-born, the Mendez family had no choice but to accept deportation. "The government should never have sent us back to Mexico," he said.

Following their forced repatriation, the Mendez family re-settled in Michoacan. Gil eventually went to live with his uncle in Monterey, where he continued his formal education until Mexico declared war on Germany in May 1942. Until then, Gil had never given much thought to Pearl Harbor. He saw it as a tragedy, to be sure, but it was an *American* problem. By this point, he had been living in Mexico for more than ten years, speaking mostly Spanish, and he thought that this new conflict would run its course without Mexico's involvement. "Mexico was very sympathetic toward the Germans at first," said Gil, "and prior to the war they did a lot of business with Germany." But when the *Kriegsmarine* started targeting Mexican ships on the high seas, the Mexican government promptly declared war on the Axis Powers. "When the Mexican President declared the war," Gil continued, "they instituted conscription, or the draft."

Gil was a few months shy of his 18th birthday, the minimum age for duty in the Mexican Armed Forces. "They called it the '1924 Class,' which was the year that I was born. They drafted everybody that was eighteen. And they used the lottery system," which ultimately selected Gilberto Mendez as one of its earliest draftees. But his uncle was quick to say: "You don't have to go because you are a United States citizen. It's up to you...but if you don't want to go, we'll go to the authorities here, and we can go to the US Consulate, and tell them the situation."

Gil thought it over.

"Well," he said, "everybody that was born in 1924 is volunteering to go. I think I'll go." After all, the designated term of service was only *one* year. Thus, Gilberto Mendez enlisted in the Mexican Army.

He was sent with his fellow conscripts to Jalisco, where they were issued their new equipment, uniforms, and rifles. "For new recruits," he said, "we were embedded with the regular army but we were separate." And at the end of his 90-day training cycle, Gil was promoted to the rank of second sergeant. "The Mexican Army only has two types of sergeants," he explained, "second sergeant and a first sergeant." His designation as "second sergeant" put him in charge of the company's administrative functions.

"We stayed six months in Guadalajara," he said. "And we used to just drill all day long...took a break for lunch, and then in the evening we'd have at least two hours of lectures, tactics, and classroom training. After six months [in September 1942], we went to Mexico City in a convoy and participated in the parade on the Sixteenth of September…Mexican Independence Day." After the parade, Gil's unit was sent to Queretaro. "We went to stay at a convent that was part of a church taken over by Benito Juarez [the famous 1800s-era Mexican president] and we spent six months there doing the same thing that we did in Guadalajara. Training, exercises, and classroom training."

Gil was discharged on Christmas Day 1942.

It was an uneventful end to a seemingly uneventful conscription. Still, his brief service in the Mexican Army taught him a lot about the fundamentals of military science. And the Mexican Armed Forces served with distinction during the war, most notably the 201st Fighter Squadron of the Mexican Air Force. Dubbed the "Aztec Eagles," these P-47 pilots were attached to the US 58th Fighter Group, flying some 96 combat missions over the Pacific.

Meanwhile, back in the States, Gil's eldest sister received an interesting letter in the mail. She had been allowed to stay in Texas because she was already married to an American citizen. "The Draft Board had gotten in touch with her," said Gil—asking for his whereabouts and demanding that he register for the draft. "Well, he's in Mexico," she told them. "He was deported with the rest of my family." But the Draft Board was clear: "If he doesn't appear within thirty days, he is going to lose his citizenship."

Gil and his family were dumbfounded.

Despite being an American citizen by birth, the US Government had cast him down to Mexico; and now they were threatening to revoke his citizenship if he didn't come back and register for the draft.

Gil didn't know what to do.

Did the US have any legal basis to revoke his citizenship? Or was it all a scare tactic?

Going to his uncle, Gil said: "I have to go back, because I might lose my citizenship if I don't." The uncle, who was likely just as perplexed as his nephew, said: "It's up to you. Whatever you want, I told your mother that I would help you." Thus, Gil Mendez returned to the US to accept conscription. He reported to the Induction Center on March 31, 1943.

"We were shipped to San Diego," he said, where he and his comrades were given their options of service. His older brother, Vincent, had joined the Navy two years earlier and was serving as an aerial photographer.

"Try to get into the Navy," his brother told him.

"At that time," said Gil, "it was supposedly the best branch of the service." Gil asked for naval service, but a Marine Corps gunnery sergeant quickly burst into the room: "I need ten volunteers," he said. "You will be Navy personnel, but you will be in the Marine Corps, which is the infantry of the Navy. And you will be the fighting force, land, sea, and air, and you will be at the disposal of the President of the United States."

The gunnery sergeant's dress blue uniform definitely added to the showmanship.

"This sounds pretty good," Gil thought to himself. "So, I was one of those volunteers." Within the next few days, he reported to Camp Pendleton in San Diego for recruit training. As he described, Marine recruits went through "boot camp" followed by "line camp." Boot camp, of course, taught the fundamentals of warfare and military life. "They just drilled you to death," he said. Line camp, however, was a more advanced level of training. "Night patrols, simulated combat against dummies," interspersed with survival training, demolitions, and anti-tank weapons.

Gil found that his prior service in the Mexican Army had prepared him well for the rigors of boot camp. Although the 1940s Mexican Army was small, Gil remembered that they were tough and highly professional. "They were very disciplined," he said. Thus, when he arrived at Camp Pendleton, "I didn't suffer because I had the discipline already embedded in me from the Mexican Army." After line camp, Gil and his fellow Marines arrived in Hawaii. "We continued more advanced training, night patrols, and [training maneuvers with] landing craft,"—the famous Higgins landing boats.

From Hawaii, they boarded a troop ship, en route to whatever Marine ground units would take them. "We were replacements," he said. None of them had yet been assigned to a unit. "We went as a 'nobody' group," he continued. "Because, as replacements, we were here…there… wherever we were needed." Such was the life of a replacement. Indeed, a replacement was sent to any unit where a fellow Marine had been killed, and would literally replace that fallen comrade in the ranks of his unit.

After a few days at sea, the troop carrier met up with an invasion convoy. Gil didn't know it at the time, but he was in the convoy headed for Iwo Jima. "Hundreds of ships," he recalled. And on February 19, 1945, Gil could see the faint silhouette of the craggy island jutting up from the horizon. "Now, the Air Force and the Navy had bombarded that island for *nineteen* consecutive days, day and night," he lamented—but they hadn't killed a thing.

The Japanese had gone underground, determined to wait out the shelling.

And now that the bombardment was over, the Rising Sun had emerged

The iconic flag raising on Iwo Jima. February 23, 1945.

from their spider holes and were ready to return fire on the incoming task force. The convoy was under fire but, as Gil recalled, "we stayed on the ship because…we were being held in reserve as replacements for the other units." Indeed, the first wave of Marines were expected to suffer heavy casualties; and they needed a steady stream of replacements to sustain the momentum of the attack.

Still, most of the Allied commanders were anticipating a quick victory on Iwo Jima. "We were told that the operation, the whole operation, would only take three to four days," Gil remembered. "And then it turned out that it was 36 days of pure hell." But during the opening rounds of the battle, Gil was more concerned with being on a big ship than being on the beaches. The troop carriers presented bigger targets; and one well-placed shot from an onshore battery could take the ship, and its Marines, to the bottom of the sea.

When the first wave of Higgins boats descended onto Iwo Jima, "all hell broke loose," said Gil. From the deck of his troop carrier, miles offshore, Gil remembered: "You could see the Higgins boats receiving direct hits, going sky high. That's when I got scared." For the next few days, he saw the muzzle flashes of American and Japanese forces flickering across the landscape, most of which were punctuated by violent explosions from the supporting artillery. He saw a glimmer of hope, however, on the fifth day of the battle. From the top of Mount Suribachi, the highest point on Iwo Jima, a group of Marines raised the American flag.

"We saw it from the ship."

Joe Rosenthal, an embedded photographer from the Associated Press, captured the moment in his iconic photograph, *Raising the Flag on Iwo Jima*. The photo itself came to represent the Pacific War, and has since become a symbol of Marine Corps heritage. But for Gil Mendez, seeing the Stars & Stripes raised in real time was a thrill like none other. "Your heart was beating a thousand times a minute," filling him with pride, and even giving him goosebumps.

After six days of waiting along the coastal waters, Gil's troop carrier finally began making its way to the shore. The beachhead had been secured, but even at D-Day +6, Gil Mendez still did not have an assigned unit. As replacements, Gil and his friends wouldn't be sorted out until they made landfall.

Wading off the Higgins boat, the new Marines assembled onto the black volcanic sand. One by one, a personnel sergeant called names from a roll sheet, assigning each new replacement to a rifle company. When Gil answered to his name, he was directed to I Company, 23d Marine Regiment (part of the 4th Marine Division).

His first week in the 23d Marines, however, was marked by feelings of dread. Statistically speaking, a GI stood the greatest chance of being killed during (a) the first few months of his tour, or (b) the last few months of his tour. And Gil Mendez didn't want to fall on the wrong side of that statistic.

In fact, he was so hypervigilant that he couldn't sleep.

He was running on pure adrenaline.

He refused to let go of his rifle, even while eating or using the latrine. "I felt that if I dropped my rifle...I would be killed." For fear of lingering snipers, he often told himself: "Gilberto, don't get up." Enemy snipers were, after all, a persistent threat. And they enjoyed taking aim at a GI's head. "And I didn't sleep because of the stink of the blown-up bodies. Bodies torn to pieces."

"Our mission was to take the main airfield," he said—the infamous Airfield One. And the Japanese were defending it with their customary fanaticism. Part of the airfield was guarded by an enormous bunker. "We called it the Meat Grinder," said Gil, "because it played hell on our troops."

Indeed, a medley of Japanese mortars, machine guns, and anti-tank guns wrought havoc on any one trying to gain access to the airfield. "They had everything they could throw," Gil added. "And they had the advantage to be close. They were on the highest part [of the hill]."

While moving forward to take the airfield, Gil's company was pinned down by heavy gunfire. "We were pinned down," he said, "for a number of hours…we couldn't move, because every time somebody got up, or exposed himself, he was gone." But during the opening rounds of this firefight, Gil had taken cover behind a thick slab of volcanic rock. "It was an act of God," he said, because the shape of the rock allowed him to prop his rifle into a good firing position, while still providing good cover from the enemy's counterfire. And, as it turned out, this rock would play a critical role in saving Gil's life. For within the next few hours, Gil Mendez would have his first encounter with a Japanese *banzai* attack.

It was about 7:00 AM, and Gil remembered that "there were about twenty of us [three infantry squads] pinned down along that section of the battlefield when we saw something glistening in the sunlight." Whatever it was, he could tell by its luster that it had a highly-reflective surface. "I thought it was a mirror," he said, "because they had showed us in line camp how to communicate with a mirror," using the reflective sunlight to flash communiques in Morse Code.

But these flashes didn't resemble any type of naval code.

In fact, they seemed erratic…and almost panicky.

That's when Gil realized it was no mirror…*it was the blade of a samurai sword.* A Japanese officer had emerged from one of the caves, rallying a group of wild-eyed soldiers behind him.

And Gil could hear them shouting: *"Banzai! Banzai!"*

By now, the bullets were flying in both directions, but Gil remained perfectly concealed behind his rock, ready to line up his first shot against the fanatical *bushido* warriors. At that moment, the fear and nerves left him; all his focus was directed into picking off the Japanese troops…one by one.

"I was shooting until I ran out of ammunition," he said. But rather than sprint back to the ammo point, "I decided to crawl." And, just as he had done during his first week on Iwo Jima, he told himself *not* to get up. "Because I had seen the bodies with shots in the head," he recalled, "they got up…they exposed themselves, and they were gone."

The mantra continued as he shimmied on his belly:

"Don't get up, Gilberto. Don't get up."

He belly-crawled over to two fellow Marines on his left, asking for a bandolier. Each of them happily obliged, tossing Gil a single bandolier. Thus, with two full bandoliers, Gil crawled back to his rock, ready to take aim at the next wave of incoming troops. "And here…the Japanese, kept on coming out of the cave."

Kneeling back behind his rock, Gil drew a bead on a Japanese soldier who was slowly cresting a rise in the terrain. At first, all he could see was the helmet, but it soon morphed into the unmistakable visage of a Japanese infantryman.

Aiming for his neck, "I pulled the trigger…pow."

But surprisingly, the enemy soldier didn't die. The bullet had only wounded him. Nearly a minute later, Gil was aghast to see this *same* soldier crawling up a rise in the terrain, "trying to push himself forward." Without hesitation, Gil readied his rifle for another shot.

"Bang! Bang! Bang! And the clip jumps up and out of the rifle."

Gil reloaded just in time to see the Japanese soldier expire. "They found thirteen holes in his body." Gil didn't know it at the time, but this was the same officer, who had led the *banzai* charge with his samurai sword. "They found his sword right beside him."

"Anyway, they kept on coming," Gil continued. "I stayed behind that rock ten hours." By the end of that firefight, however, Gil was credited with *twenty* confirmed kills. In total, the platoon had killed nearly 70 Japanese soldiers.

But this battle for Iwo Jima was far from over.

The following day, Gil recalled: "we started moving out and all hell broke loose again." Mortar fire, machinegun fire, rifle fire, an anti-tank fire pelted the American positions. Of the enemy's ordnance, the anti-tank guns seemed to be the worst. Gil described the Japanese anti-tank guns as somewhat comparable to the US 37mm pieces—deadly when used against armor *or* dismounts.

"One of the mortar shells landed pretty close to me," he said. "I was lucky because they later told me that a large piece of shrapnel was embedded in my pick shovel on my back. So, I could imagine, and anybody could imagine, had it not been for that [shovel] it would have hit me probably somewhere in the spine." Still, the impact of the mortar had been close enough to knock Gil clear off his feet—"and with a terrible ringing in my ear, my right ear."

To make matters worse, the shock wave had disrupted Gil's equilibrium to the point that he was now choking on his own tongue. A corpsman and a fellow Marine tried to pull his tongue out with a safety pin. "They pierced my tongue and they were pulling my lip," he recalled, trying to get his tongue from becoming his own demise.

"Get up," they pleaded.

But Gil couldn't even stand.

For that matter, he could hardly hear.

"And that terrible ringing in my ear," he said. "It took about six months after I was discharged to get rid of the thing." Deducing that Gil had no physical wounds, the corpsman and other Marine hoisted Gil back to the field hospital. He had obviously sustained a concussion, but they had no idea how bad it may have been. "Then a nurse came over, gave me a shot, I don't know what, but it knocked me out."

When he woke up on February 28, 1945, he was on a hospital ship bound for Hawaii.

"We were dropped off in Maui…transferred to another ship and came back to the US, to the Oakland Receiving Hospital. We stayed in Oakland just a short while, maybe a day or two. Then we joined in a convoy by bus, went from Oakland to San Diego." After a brief stay at Balboa Navy Hospital, Gilberto Mendez was honorably discharged from the Marine Corps in November 1945.

Having served in combat, while wearing the uniform of his American birthland, Gil was certain that no one could argue for a *second* deportation. In fact, he never understood the legality of why he and his parents had been deported the first time. He was, after all, an American citizen by birth. And although his parents were not citizens, they were, nevertheless, *legal* residents. But such was the nature of the great Mexican Repatriation of the 1930s.

All told, however, Gil had no desire to return to Mexico.

In November 1945, he bought a bus ticket to San Antonio, where he remained for the rest of his life. "When I was discharged, I spent about two, three days just making applications," he said. "I made applications for every government installation that there was at the time. Lackland, Kelly, Fort Sam, Randolph, Brooks [Army Hospital], everywhere, the Post Office, the VA. And the first one to call me for an interview was the Post Office, but they wanted me as a postal clerk."

Gil wasn't impressed.

"No," he said, "I want to be outside. I want to *deliver* the mail."

"Well," said the postmaster, "we don't have a position available right now, but if you want postal clerk…you'll have a job."

Gil stood his ground.

"No, I don't want to be inside. I like the outdoors."

That's when he landed a job at Lackland Air Force Base. He remained a federal employee for the next several decades until his retirement.

Reflecting on his service in both the Mexican Army and US Marine Corps, Gil said: "If I had to do it again, I would gladly do it. By the grace of God, I'm here, and I have four children. Three girls and my son…and three out of four have worn a uniform of this country. I had a daughter in the Army, my son in the Navy, [and] my youngest daughter in the Navy making a career out of her service. I think that I paid my ticket."

Gilberto Mendez passed away on April 29, 2012, at the age of 87. He was buried with military honors at Fort Sam Houston National Cemetery in San Antonio, Texas.

10
COMBAT MAILMAN
FRANK CANNEY,
AN ARMY POSTAL WORKER IN COMBAT

By the standards of conscription warfare, Frank Canney was already an "old man." At 34 years of age, he was more than a decade older than most of his fellow GIs. He had been a postal worker in California prior to answering the call of duty in 1943. Owing to his service in the US Post Office, Frank was made an Army mail handler. "A year later," he said, "I went overseas as a replacement in the Army Postal Unit of the 24th Infantry Division." The bastion of these Army postal workers was the "Army Post Office"—the ever-popular APO.

By the summer of 1944, he had served all throughout the Pacific, manning APOs in Dobodura, Wakde, and Hollandia.

And he had never heard a shot fired in anger.

All this changed, however, on the morning of October 20, 1944, when Allied forces invaded the Philippine Islands at Leyte Gulf. "My outfit, on the Liberty ship *Marcus Daily*, was shaken up when Japanese bombs hit a forward 75mm gun position," he said, "killing every member of the armed guard." Liberty ships were a class of cargo ships used to transport men and materiel to the frontlines.

Frank's unit hit the beach on October 25. "There followed two months of bombing and torrential rains while we were stationed in a Chinese-owned rice warehouse in Tacloban"—the provincial capital. From there, his APO sailed to Mindoro as part of the Western Visayan Task Force. "I was aboard LST 741," he recalled, "in a convoy of twenty-five ships." It was in this convoy, as it steamed into the Sulu Sea, that Frank Canney would have his first sustained look at the carnage of naval combat.

"Before getting underway," he said, "we GIs descended to the tank deck and secured the ambulances, Jeeps, six-bys [utility trucks], weapons carriers, and other vehicles by running heavy chains around their wheels, and attaching them firmly to the deck." Advanced elements of the 24th Infantry Division and the 503d Parachute Infantry Regiment had departed days earlier. "These were led by the ill-fated cruiser *Nashville*," he said, "carrying the Task Force commander, Brigadier General William Dunckel"—along with a bevy of other high-ranking Allied officers.

The *Nashville* had been crippled by a *kamikaze* attack on December 13, killing 133 sailors and wounding an additional 190. These *kamikaze* attacks were a fairly new (and incredibly disturbing) tactic in military aviation. Japanese pilots would deliberately ram their aircraft into the oncoming Allied ships—hoping to sink them or kill as many sailors as possible. "It was terrifyingly effective…and hard to cope with." Indeed, it showed what little regard the Imperial Japanese forces had for human life.

Frank's convoy set sail on December 19, 1944. A motley crew of Victory, Liberty, and LST ships, this convoy numbered twenty vessels in total—not including the eleven destroyers that formed their protective screen. "They darted around our flanks like nervous watch dogs," he said. "So great was their speed, sometimes reaching thirty or more knots, that when turning, their port or starboard rails almost touched the water line." For the first two nights at sea, their voyage had passed without incident. "The weather was ideal, with a calm sea marked by gentle, rolling swells."

However, Frank and his fellow GIs were not merely "passengers." Indeed, aboard every troop carrier, the soldiers were expected to be gainfully employed, helping the ship's company with their critical tasks. In that regard, Frank Canney had become an "assistant gunner" of sorts. During General Quarters, he would load ammunition into a port-side .50 cal anti-aircraft gun.

On the morning of December 21, the men aboard LST 741 had endured two calls to General Quarters, both of which had been false alarms. There had been no enemy ships on the horizon; and there had been nothing in the skies except a few scattered clouds.

But the third call to General Quarters would be the proverbial charm.

One of the destroyers spotted a seemingly out-of-place junk ship. "The junk must have been motorized, though, as it quickly sailed towards a far-off island." The destroyer gave chase, signaling for the junk to turn about. But this junk, obviously an enemy recon ship, ignored the warning and tried to flee the scene. Though small and agile, the speedy junk could neither outrun the destroyer, nor outmaneuver its gun batteries. Following a quick salvo from the forward gun battery, the junk disappeared under a cloud of billowing smoke and raging fires.

But the junk obviously had time to report their position.

LST 741, the landing craft that carried Frank Canney onto the beaches of the Philippine Islands.

For within minutes, a dozen Zeroes came thundering over the horizon, silhouetted against the red glow of the setting sun. Aboard LST 741, Canney's unit shared its billets with an Australian detachment. Wearing their signature khakis and floppy hats, Canney recalled one of them shouting "Here come the bloody Nips!" as the all-too-familiar droning of Japanese aircraft filled the air.

General Quarters sounded.

"My hands were sweaty and I had a queasy feeling in the pit of my stomach as I ran to my station. By this time, the sun was low on the western horizon and I hoped for the shelter of darkness that comes so quickly in these waters only twelve degrees above the Equator."

Sadly, it was not to be.

Almost immediately, the Japanese planes descended upon the convoy, hitting one of the more vulnerable support ships, causing it to lose its place in the convoy. "Every gun on LST 741 started firing. I carried magazines from the locker to the twin .50 while the gunner blazed away at low-flying aircraft. Soon, the air overhead was filled with ack-ack bursts." Suddenly, one of the offending Zeroes swooped down along the port side of LST 741. "My gunner and the ones nearby sprayed .50 cal rounds towards it," Frank recalled—many of which met their mark, shearing off the bandit's wing, and sending his plane headlong into the sea.

Three more planes were quickly shot down—"two of them bursting into flames"—but the third Zero had just been inspired to turn himself into a suicide bomber. Going into a long glide, the pilot set his sights on the neighboring LST 460. Frank watched in horror as the fanatical pilot plowed his Zero into the ship's main deck, crashing into the cargo hold, whereupon he detonated all the 105mm and 155mm artillery shells onboard. Within moments, LST 460 was ablaze from its bow to its stern. The artillery shells, cooking off from the intense heat, rocketed into the air, leaving a fiery trail of smoke and gunpowder in their wake.

"It seemed like a madman's Fourth of July celebration," said one sailor.

The sky was red, and parts of the sea were ablaze, as a growing mass of sailors desperately swam away from the flaming LST. But among the shell-shocked and badly-burned survivors lay several of their less fortunate comrades, bobbing face-down in the water as their lifeless bodies drifted with the current.

"I saw hundreds of sailors and soldiers leaping overboard," said Frank. Some tried to launch lifeboats while others simply threw life rafts over the side. "Some crewmen, stricken by panic," he continued, "leapt into the sea. They dropped upon the heads of other men, resulting in additional casualties." Some of the more able-bodied survivors swam towards LST 741. The skipper then ordered the ship into rescue mode.

"Now it was time for saving instead of killing," said Frank.

Hoisting the "mercy flag" up its main mast, LST 741 signaled that it was now picking up survivors. A slew of Higgins LCVP landing boats soon descended from LST 741, motoring gingerly among the mass of ill-fated sailors and GIs. Frank and his port-side comrades, meanwhile, cast lines off the rail to survivors struggling to reach 741. "We hauled up burning and screaming men," he said. "Medics and corpsmen, with many a Yank and Aussie volunteers, placed stricken survivors on litters and carried them into the wardroom for medical attention. This part of the ship was to become a combination hospital and mortuary."

Some of the men, however, were too badly wounded to climb up the lifelines under their own power. For these ailing survivors, Frank and his comrades tied belays to the strongest swimmers aboard LST 741, lowering them into the sea. The strong swimmers stayed afloat by treading water as they tied their lines under the armpits of the bobbing wounded. "They, too, were, hoisted aboard for medical care."

As LST 460 began its fiery descent into the black tepid waters, Frank noticed something peculiar—"tiny lights," as he described them, blinking on the surface of the sea. "These belonged to naval personnel swimming towards the rescue ships. Each sailor had a blinker attached to his Kapok life jacket." These pulsating lights would facilitate easier rescues during the hours of darkness.

"But what about the soldiers?" he asked himself.

Army personnel had no such beacons on their life jackets. "How could they be found when the quick tropical darkness settled over the ocean?" How many would survive until daybreak? "Hundreds of soldiers could have died," said Frank, "because the Army failed to have the foresight to put signal lights on its men's life jackets. That was one occasion where it was better to be a sailor instead of a soldier!"

The following morning, December 22, the Western Visayan Task Force made landfall at Mindoro. Frank Canney and the rest of the GIs on LST 741 landed unopposed at Red Beach. Ironically, Frank's landing party suffered only *one* casualty while storming the beach: a soldier was trampled by an angry water buffalo. "But," he said wryly, "our casualties in the sea battles had been heavy."

Frank spent the remainder of the war manning the 24th Infantry Division's APO on Mindoro. "I was stationed in the barrio of San Jose, about five miles inland." But even at the APO, he found little relief from the enemy. "Our units went through many bombings," he said, "both day and night, from the Japanese bases north of us."

But the Allies had begun clearing their own landing strips on Mindoro, and their combined air forces were determined to give as much as they had gotten. The closest airstrip to the APO was occupied by the Royal

Australian Air Force—running daily sorties of Aussie and American aircraft. Their ranks included B-24 Liberators; P-47 Thunderbolts; P-51 Mustangs; P-38 Lightnings; and a squadron of P-61 Black Widows (deadly night fighters); and US Marine F4U Corsairs. Frank remembered that this aerial armada was highly effective in clearing the way for the upcoming invasion of Luzon.

Christmas Day 1944 was as enjoyable a holiday as one could have in the forward area of Mindoro. "Filipinos from the surrounding barrios were invited to share a feast of roast turkey, mashed potatoes, gravy, pie and coffee," said Frank. "We filled our mess kits and our cups, talking about how fortunate we had been so far." Even in light of the carnage they had witnessed on the high seas, Frank and his fellow GIs were grateful not to have endured the meat grinder battles or Tarawa, Saipan, and the Mariana Islands.

"But our luck was too good to last."

The very next day, Allied Intelligence detected a Japanese naval task force headed straight for Mindoro—"a cruiser and two destroyers."

Under the cover of darkness, the 24th Division and the 503d Parachute Infantry started digging in near the beach. "Those of us in the rear echelon outfits received orders to fall back to the inland hills." Frank grabbed his hammock along with as many C and K Rations as his shoulder pack could carry. With a full clip of ammunition for his carbine, he began the long hill-ward march to the high ground of Mindoro.

Trudging along the narrow roads under the bright moonlight, Frank saw a caravan of ambulances and supply trucks pass him by, vehicles belonging to the 2d Field Hospital and the 13th Station Hospital. If and when the enemy hit the beach, these medics would be the first support soldiers dispatched to the shores of Mindoro. Behind them were a steady stream of Filipino refugees, eager to avoid the anticipated bombardment. "Many of these Filipinos, most of them loyal to the Americans, had been through this kind of exodus before," Frank remembered. The Japanese had forced many from their homes in 1942; the Filipinos then returned jubilantly to the beaches when the Western Visayan Task Force arrived; now they were on the move again to take shelter farther inland. "Hundreds of refugees passed us," carrying what few possessions they owned. "One boy held a bicycle frame by an arm. Others trundled wheelbarrows and small carts, filled with everything from cooking utensils to blankets and small carts."

After nearly an hour into their march, Frank and the others heard the sound of aircraft overhead. It couldn't have been Allied, as their own

The ill-fated LST 450, which came under fire and sank in route the Philippines. Frank Canney witnessed the ship's demise from his position aboard LST 741.

fighters and bombers had taken flight from Mindoro to search for the enemy fleet. Frank's suspicions were confirmed when a Japanese spotter plane began dropping flares above the tree line.

"We hit the ditch," he said.

A young lieutenant came into view.

"Pass the word," he told Frank. "Watch out for enemy paratroops."

After dropping more flares over the island, the Japanese recon plane returned to sea, likely to be picked up by the incoming cruiser. "We clicked the safeties off our carbines, holding them in readiness for the enemy's next move."

Paratroopers?

Aerial bombardment?

An amphibious landing?

The GIs wouldn't have to wait long to find out. For within moments, Frank was greeted by the rushing, crackling sound of incoming naval shells. "I had been under much strafing and bombing," he said, "but this was the first time that I experienced heavy shellfire from a battle cruiser and two destroyers."

But the shelling stopped almost as soon as it had started.

"For over an hour, we stayed in the ditch, relieved by the silence and total darkness." After getting the "All Clear," Frank and his comrades were ordered to move back down towards the beach.

"The next morning, I learned that American and Australian forces had been saved by our PT boats." The prowling PTs had crept up on the Japanese task force undetected. "They dropped their torpedoes and sped away into the night…putting the destroyers out of action and seriously damaging the armored warship [cruiser]. That was my experience under fire."

Frank Canney remained on Mindoro until December 1945, three and a half months after Japan's formal surrender. While loading his APO back aboard the troop ship, he beheld a poignant, yet saddening sight. At the temporary Allied cemetery, a Graves Registration unit was digging up the bodies of the men who had lost their lives during the convoy sea battles en route to Mindoro, "and also during the subsequent bombings and the one night of shellfire." Dead or alive, every member of the Western Visayan Task Force was going home.

Frank Canney returned to the United States on January 2, 1946. He was honorably discharged from the United States Army shortly thereafter. He and his wife, Lauretta, settled in Salinas, California, where he returned to his job with the US Postal Service. He was happily employed as a letter carrier for the next several years, until he earned his eligibility for retirement. He passed away in 1990.

11
ONE HALF ACRE OF HELL

AVIS DAGIT SCHORER WITH THE
56TH EVACUATION HOSPITAL IN ANZIO

Avis Dagit was one of eleven children growing up on a farm in Iowa. "With all those kids," she said, "you just can't stay at home." Thus, after graduating from high school in 1937, she went to Des Moines for nurse training at the Methodist Hospital. She took readily to the medical profession, and signed an agreement with the American Red Cross, pledging her service to the country if a war or other "crisis" erupted. "With Europe already at war," she said, "and the world situation deteriorating, that crisis seemed likely."

And the crisis finally arrived on December 7, 1941.

"I knew on December 7," she said, "that I was all in." Following the attack on Pearl Harbor, Avis took the next four months to settle her personal affairs before reporting to the Army Induction Center in Des Moines on March 17, 1942—her 23d birthday.

Sworn into the ranks of the Army Nurse Corps, Avis was commissioned as a Second Lieutenant. But she and her fellow nurses received no formal basic training. They simply went to work...and were expected to learn Army customs along the way. "You had to learn as you go," she said. "It was a whole new language for me. I'd never heard of a latrine, or a chow line, or a mess hall."

Reporting to Camp Chaffee, Arkansas, she was quickly assigned to the infirmary. But, at this early stage in the war, Camp Chaffee was a faint wisp of a military post. "When we got there, it was nothing but a few scattered buildings and some dirt roads," she said. "Not long afterwards, though, the troops started pouring in." Indeed, within a year, its ranks had swollen to more than 100,000 troops, and the Camp Hospital had grown to a 1,000-bed capacity. "It was unbelievable how quickly it developed." Years later, Camp Chaffee would become the primary hub for Cuban refugees during the Mariel Boatlift of 1980.

While learning the art of military nursing, Avis and her comrades were ordered not to fraternize with enlisted men. "But that was easily broken," she said. "Some women broke it just to see if they could get away with it." Still, the Army Nurses were happy to be part of the Regular Army, not the Women's Army Corps (WACs). "We didn't want to be called WACs." During World War II, each branch of the military had its own segregated service for females. The Army had its WACs; the Navy had its WAVES; the Army Air Forces had their WASPS; the Coast Guard had SPARS; and the Marines had their Women's Reserve.

Still, her duties at Fort Chaffee were strenuous, and often heartbreaking. "I remember one time a soldier was brought into my ward with pneumonia. We didn't have antibiotics in those days, and the head nurse told me I should report to this other ward when the soldier died. Well, I was determined he wasn't going to die on my watch, and I stayed with him for several nights. He finally did recover." But soon thereafter, another soldier in her ward died from pneumonia. "You learned that soldiers didn't have to get shot up to die," she said. "They died just from going out on maneuvers."

In February 1943, the nurses at Camp Chaffee were ordered to Fort Sam Houston, Texas, where they joined the 56th Evacuation Hospital—"made up mainly of doctors and nurses from Baylor University." The 56th was a motley crew of 48 direct-commission doctors, 49 nurses, and 310 enlisted medics. It was, however, a self-contained and self-sufficient unit, with its own x-rays, laboratories, cots, and shelter tents. Being from the Midwest, Avis quickly learned that Texans had a culture all their own. "They're so proud of their state. I sure learned all the songs of Texas," she chuckled.

Two months later, the 56th Evacuation Hospital loaded its medical gear and personnel onto a troop ship in New York City. "They didn't tell us where we were going, but when they started teaching us the language and customs of North Africa, it became pretty clear. We landed in Casablanca." In the spring of 1943, Allied forces were chasing Rommel out of North Africa. It was a hard-fought campaign, during which the US Army paid a heavy price before turning the tides against Rommel and his *Afrika Korps*.

When the 56th Evacuation Hospital arrived in-theater, they boarded a truck convoy for an eight-day trip to the front. "It was not a nice ride," Avis recalled. "It was hot, and we had to carry our own food, which was C-rations. We got a quart of water every day. There were no baths, there

Avis D. Schorer, Army Nurse.

were no slit trenches, and there was no sightseeing." But as the convoy rode onward, Avis began seeing the unmistakable signs of war. "Shell holes…blown-up tanks and vehicles littered the landscape."

The 56th eventually reached Bizerte, Tunisia, where they set up shop in an old French colonial garrison. "One night," Avis remembered, "there was an air raid." But because it was nearly July 4th, Avis and her fellow nurses cheered the bomb blasts "like it was a fireworks display," she added. "But then hundreds of casualties started coming in."

After that, the nurses weren't cheering anymore.

Several more of these early casualties were victims of malaria. "Those were some of the sickest men I've ever seen in my life." Luckily, most made a full recovery with the proper intake of atabrine.

As Avis soon found out, duty in the field hospital was exhausting work. She worked 12-hour shifts, with frequent day-night shift differentials. "As the front moved, the hospital units would leapfrog over each other." The hospitals closest to the front would treat the most casualties, while the hospitals in the rear would be able to rest and refit before rotating back to the front. But even during their so-called "rest cycles," there were plenty of casualties that needed treating. The GIs coming in from the battlefield had some of the worst injuries Avis had ever seen—burned flesh, severed limbs, missing scalps, bullet holes, and the like.

By September 1943, Avis's unit had been tapped for duty in Italy. "The Italians had surrendered by that time," she said, "and some thought we might be going on a sightseeing tour, but the Germans didn't give up and they were there to meet us." Avis and her comrades waded ashore at Salerno, and got back to work. "From that point on, we usually just wore coveralls. We had long ago forgotten about the white shoes and white dresses. We wore what the men were wearing." And by the time Avis's unit had set up at Avellino, "our tents were overflowing with the wounded." The fighting among the surrounding hills was *that* bad.

Treating the casualties (even those who had no chance to survive) was hard enough. But the oncoming winter made their job even worse. As Allied forces pressed on towards Rome: "It rained and rained…for days on end. It was muddy everywhere, and all the tents leaked. We waded in mud wherever we went. The casualties began to change as the men came in with trench foot. If they had been wounded, they were caked with mud and blood. It was a terrible situation."

But little did Avis know that the collective situation was about to get worse.

In January 1944, their hospital was ordered to prepare for the invasion of Anzio. The Allies were determined to end-run the German forces by landing behind their positions. "We boarded a British LCI at night, and were put down in a [cargo] hold. Our bathroom was a bucket in the middle of the floor. With that, and with the fumes from the ship, you could hardly get your breath. We had no blankets. Some of the nurses got sick just at the sight of the ship. I didn't, but it was miserable. The seas were vicious and tossed us around like a cork. Some of the nurses would just throw up in their helmets…lie on their bunks and moan and groan."

At one point during the trip, the nurses were offered a chance to transfer from the British LCI onto another ship. Twenty-six of the nurses who were healthy enough to do so (i.e., those not rendered immobile from seasickness), made the hasty rope ladder transfer. This second ship was more stable, but it was laden with several tons of explosives and high-octane gas. Adding to the tension (and the fear of riding aboard a floating powder keg), these nurses endured a 36-hour air raid, with Axis bombs landing within mere feet of the ship. And when the ship made landfall, these same nurses found themselves running ashore onto a beachhead that was still under enemy fire.

Still, these 26 ladies were the first nurses to land on Anzio.

Scrambling off the beach, the nurses got a few miles inland before a male officer stopped them: "What are you women doing here? This place is hot. Get out of here!"

Avis later described her arrival in Anzio as a nightmare. "I'm sure that anybody who was at Anzio has it seared in their minds forever. It was just crazy. We were so tired. We'd had no sleep for several days." And the Nazis weren't going to let the GIs take Anzio without a fight. "The Germans had this long-range gun we called the Anzio Express," she continued. "It had a screeching sound and it just got louder and louder as it approached. Your heart would stop until you heard it hit on the other side. You'd be relieved, but then you'd realize that it probably hit somebody else."

Meanwhile, getting the 56th consolidated was a chore unto itself. "The task was made more difficult because the unit had been split up on five different landing ships." But as soon as the 56th Evacuation Hospital opened for business, it was flooded by the onrush of casualties. "It was much worse than anything we had seen before. Instead of one wound, these men would have multiple wounds." Because the 56th was so close to the front, they saved many a soldiers' lives. But despite their prominent Red Cross markings, the hospital itself was frequently under attack. As Avis recalled: "The hospital was surrounded by fuel dumps...ammo dumps and motor pools"—making it a prime target for the *Luftwaffe* and German artillery. "The bombing was constant," she continued, "and the night was often lit up brighter than sunshine by those white flares. Sometimes, when the men were brought in, they'd ask to be allowed to go back to their foxholes where it was safer. There wasn't much protection in a tent."

To make matters worse, there was a shortage of blood, which precipitated the doctors, nurses, and medics of the 56th to donate their own blood on a regular basis. Still, Avis and her fellow nurses worked at breakneck speed to heal the ever-growing influx of casualties. "We got their wounds cleaned and did some operations," she said. "We watched out for gas gangrene and other complications. Our goal was to get them into a condition where it was safe to move them."

But no one was truly safe at Anzio...not even the nurses.

In fact, six of her fellow nurses were killed on Anzio Beach, including one of Avis's close friends whom she had known from the Methodist Hospital in Des Moines. "She was killed in an air raid. It was dreadful, but you didn't have time to break down. Your attitude was: 'Well, this is going to happen to all of us.'"

Ironically, one of their only sources of entertainment was listening to Axis Sally. Despite the anti-American broadcasts, Hitler's propaganda DJ actually played the best music. One day between songs, however, Axis

Sally said that there would soon be "happy days" for the 56th Evacuation Hospital. Avis didn't know what to make of the remark. How did Sally know about their unit? And who had told her? Moreover, what did she mean by "happy days?" Were the Germans planning a massive counteroffensive? Was the hospital itself on the target list?

"We didn't know what she was talking about; but the next day, we were relieved [from duty in Anzio]."

Avis and her comrades had been on the Anzio beachhead for a grueling 76 days. During that time, she had seen some of the worst carnage of the war. "It sounds crazy, but we didn't want to leave. We didn't want to be called quitters."

But alas, the 56th Evacuation Hospital had no choice in the matter. They were rotated off Anzio Beach and sent south to the Cassino front—just in time to treat casualties from the Battle of Monte Cassino. On June 6, 1944, however, the Allies entered Rome. "But it was kind of an anticlimax," she said. "The D-Day landings happened the same day. We were all so excited."

Still, it was a long road ahead for the Americans fighting in the Italian campaign. Indeed, as the 56th moved farther along the Italian Peninsula, they began seeing evidence of another deadly weapon—land mines. "Some of the mines would blow off a foot, but they also had these 'Bouncing Betties.' They were vicious things. They would kill and maim the civilians, the children, even the farm animals."

Towards the end of 1944, the hospital crossed the Arno River and moved into Florence. The following spring, the Allies made their final push into the Po Valley. "I don't think one square foot of that valley didn't have a shell hole or bomb crater in it. But it was a gorgeous spring, and the German Army was finally beginning to disintegrate. They were giving up by the thousands." Soon, too, would Adolf Hitler—although he elected suicide over capture. Hitler's death was a clarion call for the 56th. In many ways, Hitler's demise took the edge off the grief they shared over President Roosevelt's death earlier that month. "Roosevelt died and it was very traumatic. It was just devastating to lose him."

A week after Hitler's suicide, however, the German Army surrendered and the news of V-E Day rang throughout the world. By this time, the 56th Evacuation Hospital had spent 25 months in theater, and had seen more than 73,000 patients. With the war in Europe effectively over, Avis and her friends were excited to be going home.

"But as usual, the Army had other plans."

Her unit was sent to Udine, Italy, near the Yugoslavian border. And there was muffled talk of a pending deployment to Japan. Fortunately, the Japanese surrendered in September 1945, and the 56th Evacuation redeployed to the US that October. She was discharged from the Army Nurse Corps in February 1946, completing nearly four years of active service.

Reflecting on her wartime service, Avis said: "When you're going through something, sometimes you just can't comprehend it all. You just take it a day at a time and hope later you can sort it all out." Even during her later years, Avis's memories remained sharp. "I can still see the faces that I saw then. They still flash in front of you."

Returning to civilian life, Avis went back to school on the GI Bill, receiving her certification as a nurse anesthetist. In 1950, she married Dr. Calvin Schorer (a fellow GI), with whom she had three children. She worked at hospitals in Detroit and Iowa City before moving to Minneapolis in 1968. She became one of the leading nurse anesthetists at Lutheran Deaconess Hospital until her retirement in 1982.

Avis later wrote of her experiences in the book, *A Half Acre of Hell*, initially as a project for her children. And like many other projects in life, Avis attacked the book with a great sense of purpose. Still in print, the book has continued to garner positive reviews. "I was surprised," she admitted. "I never had any idea anybody would find it interesting except my family."

Avis Dagit Schorer passed away on August 31, 2016 at the age of 97.

12
GROUND ZERO: GUADALCANAL

Bob Johnson,
A Marine Artillery Officer in the South Pacific

Bob Johnson was a hero of the college gridiron. From 1936-38, he played defensive tackle for the University of Minnesota—two seasons punctuated by a National Championship and two Big Ten Conference titles. In fact, during one game against Washington State in 1937, he ran an interception for some 86 yards. Despite these impressive plays, however, professional football would not be in his future. Instead, he graduated with a business degree, and began the arduous task of looking for work in Depression-era Minnesota. "The only job I could find was as a grease monkey down at the Standard station in Anoka [his hometown]. I decided to look for something else."

Thus, he enrolled at the University of Minnesota School of Law, where he befriended future US Marine and Minnesota Governor, Orville Freeman. While learning the art of jurisprudence, Bob was shocked to hear of the attack on Pearl Harbor. Both he and Orville had registered for the draft, and both men knew that they had high lottery numbers— meaning that they stood a high chance of being drafted into the first wave of conscripts. Given the severity of Pearl Harbor, and the realization that America would be fighting a two-front war, Bob and Orville had a choice: They could wait to be drafted, or leave school and join voluntarily.

They chose the latter.

"If we were going to fight, we wanted to fight with an outfit that knew how to fight. So, we both joined the Marines."

Upon his induction, Bob was sent to Quantico, Virginia for Officer Candidate School, with follow-on training at Camp Elliott in San Diego. As one of several "shake-and-bake" Marine officers—hastily trained to meet manpower needs—he was assigned as the Executive Officer (XO) of an artillery battery in the 10th Marine Regiment, 2d Marine Division.

The battery's standard weapon was the pack howitzer—"a 75mm cannon that could be dissembled and moved by hard work from place to place, even in the jungle."

In the summer of 1942, the Marine Expeditionary Force deployed to the South Pacific. Bob's unit made the voyage, unescorted, aboard a commercial sea liner. Their first stop was New Zealand, where they trained in the mountains near Wellington. "We tried to make the training as realistic as possible," he said. "When we got into combat, it was a different animal altogether." Their eventual destination would be Guadalcanal.

It was America's first major offensive of the war, fought mostly by GIs with "too little experience and too little training."

Still, Guadalcanal would be the first step on the bloody road to Tokyo. Barring the exception at Midway, the Japanese had seen nothing but success throughout 1942. In May, however, a system of "Coastwatchers" (set up by the Australian Defence Force), reported to the Allies that the Japanese were building an airbase on Guadalcanal, a small island on the western edge of the Solomons. "Such an airbase would extend the Japanese ability to attack to the west, and threaten the major sea lanes to Australia." Thus came the idea for Operation Watchtower, the plan to retake Guadalcanal and capture the enemy airbase. "Because of the low priority of the Pacific campaign, compared to Europe, the operation became known to those involved as Operation Shoestring."

The 1st Marine Division led the charge, landing on Guadalcanal in August 1942. "The Marines were ashore, but they were on their own. There was no air support or sea support, and every day their four-mile beachhead was attacked from the air and shelled from passing Japanese ships." Nevertheless, the beleaguered Marines captured the airfield. By August 20, the first American planes touched down on Guadalcanal. The Japanese, meanwhile, fled into the jungle, determined to regroup and drive the Allies back into the sea.

The arrival of American air support was fortuitous, since the Japanese were planning to retake the airfield. Indeed, that night, a 1,000-man enemy task force set ashore at Taivu Point. "Either out of supreme overconfidence...or a gross underestimation of the US strength, the Japanese attacked immediately in the dead of night. The result was disastrous. By morning, 800 Japanese were dead, and their commander killed himself." The following month, the Battle of Bloody Ridge was almost just as costly. Although the Japanese had pushed the American lines back to within a thousand yards of the airfield, the Marines dug in and beat back the enemy advance.

Bob Johnson (center, wearing lip balm) poses with his fellow artillerymen on Guadalcanal.

In November 1942, Bob's unit with the 2d Marine Division landed at Guadalcanal. "We were there to relieve the troops that were on the line," he said. "The airfield had been secured by then, and it was our job to drive the Japs off the island." But the Americans' slapdash training, and their atrophied supply system, was now coming back to haunt them. Indeed, on one of Bob's first missions, he recalled: "Our maps were so bad, we couldn't use them. I went up ahead to be a forward observer so we could hit what we were supposed to hit. Sometime later, I realized I was two or three hundred yards away from our troops."

Moreover: "We seemed to always be short on supplies, and there was a constant food shortage. Our cook used to go down to one of the little bays and toss in a hand grenade. We'd have plenty of fish for supper." The Marines also scavenged barrels of rice that came floating ashore. "The rice was cast off Japanese ships for their own troops, but the troops' location had been miscalculated."

As an artillery unit, Bob's battery didn't have quite the same frontline exposure as the infantry…but the cannoneers' lives were far from easy. "I remember it was very hot, and it rained all the time. I don't think we ever got mail." Sometimes, it seemed that the local insects posed a greater threat than the Japanese. There were mosquitos, flies, leeches…and other creepy crawlers that most GIs had never heard of. In fact, during his time on Guadalcanal, more Marines died from malaria than enemy fire.

But nothing could have prepared him for the brutality (and borderline insanity) of a Japanese *banzai* attack. Bob witnessed three separate *banzai* attacks during his time in the Marine Corps, the first of which happened on Guadalcanal. "The Japanese would get all sake'd up as the night went on," he said. Saké was their drink of choice - an alcoholic beverage that, even when diluted, could lead to a quick state of inebriation. "Then they would charge en masse, yelling '*banzai*,' and screaming like you've never heard before."

That *banzai* attack came about 3:00 in the morning.

In fact, at one point during the battle, Bob's artillerymen had to lower their gun tubes, and fire their howitzers directly into the advancing enemy. "The resourcefulness of our men was incredible," he said. "I didn't have to give one order. They knew what to do. The fuses were set for the minimum and we just kept firing. I don't know how many rounds we fired." But by the end of the attack, some 300 Japanese soldiers lay dead, killed senselessly in a fit of drunken rage. "*Banzai* attacks are not something you learn about growing up on a farm outside of Anoka."

But this *banzai* charge wouldn't be his last near-brush with death. One day, the Marine howitzer crews noticed a group of heavy bombers flying overhead. Because the Americans had already taken the airfield on Guadalcanal, Bob and his fellow artillerymen assumed that the planes were Allied. "As they got close, though, all of a sudden we could see the Rising Sun on the bombers," followed by the dreadful opening of their bomb bay doors. "You can't believe how fast we got into our foxholes.

They bombed the daylights out of us, but not one guy got hurt."

Another near-death experience occurred during an unassuming Jeep ride. "The Japanese would send planes over regularly and we got to know them," he remembered. "One was 'Washing Machine Charlie,' and you could tell by the putt-putt-putt of its engine [likely a Nakajima A6M2-N or Aichi E13A]. All we had was rifle fire, and I told our guys not to even bother to shoot at him. It was just wasted ammunition. The other plane that would come over was known as 'Pistol Pete' [also a nickname given to the Japanese Type 92 artillery]. The driver and I were near the beach went Pistol Pete flew over. We watched as a couple of bombs hit nearby, with the second one closer than the first."

Bob turned to his driver, intending to tell him to vector off the road.

Bob Johnson, during his later years as an attorney. Bob continued litigating cases well into his 80s.

But before he could even get the words out, the third bomb landed next to the Jeep.

"I'll never know if I dove out of the Jeep, or if I was blown out of it," he said. All he knew was that, when he regained consciousness, he was still alive. "I wasn't injured except my ear drum was blown out. I was worried about the driver, and it turned out he was cut up pretty badly. The Jeep was destroyed."

Before Bob left Guadalcanal, he took part in a memorial service for the thousands who had died on the island. Among the seemingly endless rows of white crosses, he was startled and saddened to find a familiar name. It belonged to one of his former roommates and best friends from the University of Minnesota. "I didn't even know he had gone into the service," he said, "but it turns out he had joined the Army Air Corps and had been shot down. That shook me up a little bit."

The 2d Marine Division returned to New Zealand to rest, re-fit, and conduct more training. Thereafter, Bob Johnson fought his way through *three* additional Pacific battles—Tarawa, Saipan, and Tinian. Each island was its own brand of Hell. Tarawa, as he recalled was the worst landing. Naval Intelligence had miscalculated the tides, and the Marines had to wade through neck-high water as the onshore batteries cut them down. Saipan, however, was a personal nightmare. On his way to the beachhead, Bob's amtrack took a direct hit, wounding him and several others. "There was blood all over the place. It was just spurting out of my arm. It must have hit an artery."

When the ailing amtrack got to the shore, Bob ordered his Marines to get out, "but they were hesitating," he said. "I got to the front and dove out, and as I dove, a hand grenade went over my right head into the amtrack. I landed right on top of the Jap who had thrown the grenade. I had to get rid of him, that's all I knew." Bob killed that enemy soldier on the spot. "I've never talked about that at all until a few years ago."

As the Marines stormed Saipan, Bob was evacuated to a hospital ship, where they treated his arm and found a piece of shrapnel lodged in the cranial nerve of his neck. "I got patched up and rejoined my outfit a few days later."

Bob was preparing for the invasion of Japan when Emperor Hirohito announced the surrender in late August 1945. As part of the Occupation detail, Bob was sent to Kyushu, the southernmost Japanese island, where he went from town to town, "accepting the surrender of the local militia."

After the war, he returned to law school and was accepted to the Minnesota State Bar. Rekindling his friendship with Orville Freeman, the two served as 'Best Man" at each other's weddings. His graduation from the University of Minnesota's Law School was the start of a long and distinguished legal career. In 1948, he became a municipal judge; and from 1950-82 he was the Anoka County District Attorney. Even during his later years, he refused to retire. After leaving the DA's office, he entered private practice, where he continued litigating cases well into his 80s. When asked, at age 81, if he ever intended to retire, he simply shrugged and said: "I just come to work every day. I enjoy it."

But time eventually caught up to Bob Johnson. After a long and fulfilling legal career, he passed away in November 2010, at the age of 93.

13
COMMANDO KELLY

CHARLES E. KELLY,
MEDAL OF HONOR RECIPIENT

O n June 30, 1957, Charles E. Kelly appeared on an episode of *The Mike Wallace Interview*. Wallace opened his segment with the following monologue:

"My guest tonight was a hero of the Second World War. He's Commando Kelly, winner of the Congressional Medal of Honor, whose exploits included killing forty Germans within twenty minutes in the Battle of Salerno. Charles "Commando" Kelly, in just one of his battles, manned machine guns, rifles, and an anti-tank gun in a virtual single-handed defense of an ammunition dump and emerged unscratched. But in peacetime, Commando's been hit hard by bad-luck, ill-health, and financial misfortune."

Although hardly a dignified set-up, Charles Kelly nonetheless conducted himself with grace and poise throughout the interview. He had earned the nation's highest award for valor, but was quick to point out: "I don't think I deserve any more than any other GI just because I won the Medal of Honor. That don't make me a hero, it was just something that had to be done, and I was one of the fortunate ones."

Charles Kelly was born on September 23, 1920 in the working-class suburbs of Pittsburgh. As a kid from the "wrong side of the tracks," he spent most of his youth in a local street gang, and had numerous run-ins with the law. Despite his background as a juvenile delinquent, however, Kelly was accepted for military service in May 1942. By the following year, he was a corporal serving in the 143d Infantry Regiment, 36th Infantry Division.

In September 1943, Kelly's unit (L Company, 3d Battalion) was preparing to invade Salerno. The North African campaign had been a resounding success, and the Allies had just conquered Sicily. Taking Salerno would be the next step to conquering the Italian mainland, and getting a toehold on the European continent. Adding to the sense of good fortune was Italy's surrender on September 8, 1943. Hoping to exploit the newfound surrender, the Allies began their initial strike on Salerno the following day.

The Nazis, however, had anticipated their arrival.

They knew, as the Allies did, that the Gulf of Salerno was a critical crossroads between Sicily and Sardinia, the latter of which had just been vacated by the Axis.

Moreover, the Nazis had anticipated Italy's defection to the Allies. Although Mussolini and a few of his hardcore loyalists stayed within the Axis fold, creating the Italian Socialist Republic (an *ad hoc* splinter state), it would do nothing to stem the tide of an Allied invasion. As such, Field Marshal Albert Kesselring had the 16th Panzer Division dig in along the shores of Salerno, lying in wait for the Allied task force.

That morning of September 9, Charles Kelly waded ashore with other elements of the 36th Division. As he slogged inland, Kelly beheld the sight of his first fallen comrade: "A dead GI lying peacefully, as if asleep, with his head on his pack, his rifle by his side."

He averted his gaze, trying not to let the sight of a dead comrade faze him.

After clearing their way around a drainage ditch, Kelly's platoon met the raking gunfire of a German machine gun nest.

Kelly ducked to the ground as the whizzing bullets arced over his head.

He had narrowly escaped a premature death, but his staff sergeant hadn't been so lucky. "He went down with bullets in his head," recalled Kelly. To make matters worse, during the chaos of maneuvering around the machine gun nest, Kelly got separated from his unit.

Trying not to panic, he remembered the all-encompassing advice from his unit's leadership: "When you get on the beach, keep moving forward." It was enough to give any disoriented soldier a sense of direction. In wartime, it wasn't uncommon for soldiers to be separated from their units in the fog of combat. Thus, a general direction might help re-orient them towards an eventual rendezvous.

Taking his Browning Automatic Rifle (BAR) with him, Kelly followed a path until he came upon another group of GIs. They were mixed in from among two other companies in the regiment, and they were likely in the same situation as Kelly—separated from the main body

Charles E. Kelly.

of their respective units.

"Once more, I started looking for my outfit."

Striking down a new path, Kelly stumbled upon an abandoned farmhouse, picking peaches and grapes off the vine to satiate his hunger and stop the flow of adrenaline. "I figured I had walked about eight hours and must be about twelve miles inland." Factoring both the time and relative distance travelled, Kelly knew that he was likely in the vicinity of "Mountain 42"—a critical piece of high ground that his unit was expected to occupy. But before he could regain his bearings, he spotted a German Panzer IV rumbling down the road.

Diving into a nearby ditch, Kelly took aim and fired his BAR at the tank's slit openings. Of course, his 7.62mm bullets had no effect on the Panzer. And the Germans didn't even seem to notice that Kelly was shooting at them. Considering the noise of the tank's engine, and the mechanical droning from within the turret, the Panzer crew likely never heard the gunfire. "They rumbled and clanged by," he said, "and I kept walking down the highway, coming at last to a little creek, where I drank, took my shoes off, and bathed my feet."

While wringing out his socks, he suddenly spied the outline of Mountain 42. While hiking in the direction of the distant crag, he came upon a winery that, from what he could see, was now occupied by his regiment's 1st Battalion. Elated to have found a friendly unit, he knew that his own battalion had to be nearby. He briefly considered walking up to the 1st Battalion outpost. Surely, one of them would know where 3d Battalion had settled.

But as he drew nearer to the 1st Battalion foxholes, he quickly changed his mind.

These soldiers were a little too trigger-happy.

"They were shooting at sounds and dimly-seen movements," he said. Not the time for a social call. And certainly not the time to become a "friendly fire" statistic. Still, he couldn't blame them for being jittery. "Both sides had infiltrated into and behind each other," he said, "so that you had to be on alert each minute and watch every moving thing on each side of you." Rather than risk spooking his comrades, Kelly crawled under a nearby bush and got some sleep.

The next morning, he started down the highway, searching for anything that resembled a cluster of GIs. "It would have been nice to fill my canteen with water," he said, "but my canteen had picked up a bullet hole somewhere along the way." As he ambled down the country highway, German gunfire punctuated the long hours of silence, and Kelly eventually found his unit. As he recalled, they were "dug in among scattered, shallow holes"—hastily-prepared fighting positions dug into the countryside, waiting for the next wave of German counterattacks.

"Where the hell have you been?" they greeted him.

As it turned out, L Company had taken a tremendous beating. By the time Kelly rejoined their ranks at Mountain 42, they had been taking heavy artillery fire for the past few days. By now, the growing list of casualties had taken its toll on the unit's morale. The surviving soldiers now envied the dead. When Kelly reported to his platoon leader at Mountain 42, the lieutenant's only words were: "I sure wish they'd got you." Even among the officers, the better-off-dead mentality had infected the ranks.

Defeatist and Doomsday attitudes notwithstanding, Kelly and his comrades knew they had a job to do. "After a time, we started down the road," he said, en route to their next objective. As a rank-and-file soldier, Kelly often knew little about the broader context of their movements. When orders came to occupy a new piece of terrain, or move a certain number of miles inland, he did so without question. As they displaced from their foxholes, and marched tactically down the road, Kelly and his friends soon came upon a little Italian boy. But from the look on his face, they could see that this young boy was frightened and agitated.

"Germans! Germans! Germans!"

One of Kelly's friends who spoke fluent Italian tried to calm the boy, hoping to get more information on the whereabouts of these purported Germans. "But the kid was frightened and didn't make much sense," said Kelly. But just then, the lieutenant saw the Germans to which this boy had been referring.

"Here come some Heinie scout cars!" he shouted. "Get off the road!"

Kelly dove for cover as the enemy scout cars (likely Sd.Kfz wheeled variants) opened fire. The Americans returned fire, and two of Kelly's friends were hit. "All of a sudden, one of our boys got his bazooka on his shoulder," said Kelly, "and let go with a tremendous, crashing 'Boom!'" As the bazooka round drilled into the first enemy scout car, another GI jumped onto a nearby wall, leaping atop the second scout car, dropping his hand grenade into its crew compartment. That second car then shimmied to a halt.

The other scout vehicles quickly sped up, trying to envelop the dismounted GIs. The German crews might have succeeded, if not for a nearby anti-tank platoon. Indeed, one of 3d Battalion's anti-tank units had set up their 57mm recoilless rifles, and were taking aim at the incoming recon vehicles. "It was chancy stuff," said Kelly, "for if that 57mm had missed its target, it would have gotten us." But the anti-tank gunners engaged the remaining mounts with deadly accuracy. "The bazooka kept on booming, and, quicker than it seemed possible, that whole small reconnaissance detachment was knocked out. The place was a shambles. Scout cars were going up in flames. Tires were burning with a rubbery stink, and bodies were burning too." Kelly recalled one German leaping out from his disabled vehicle, attempting to flee the battlefield. "When we went after him," said Kelly, "he put his revolver to his head and killed himself. We had thought that only the Japs did that, and for a moment I was surprised and shocked."

But these feelings of shock soon gave way to what Kelly described as a "deep-rooted GI habit"—they started collecting souvenirs. One of his friends wrangled a German Luger; others were happy to find knives, insignias, and German Reichsmark notes. "Looking back at it," he recalled, "I can remember no feeling about the German dead except curiosity. We were impersonal about them; to us they were just bundles of rags."

About two hours later, Kelly and his unit moved into another nearby town. "The townspeople were out waving at us and offering us water, wine, and fruit," he said. Kelly also remembered it was the first time he had seen an Italian jail. "A woman had told us it was where they kept the Fascist sympathizers. The leading Fascist citizen of the town was in there, mad as blazes, and yelling his head off behind the bars."

Later that night, Kelly's platoon sergeant organized a mission to the nearby town of Altavilla. Division intelligence estimated a sizeable German contingent operating within the vicinity. "See that town over there?" said the platoon sergeant. "That's where I'm going, and I want some volunteers to go with me. I'm taking the second platoon and some sixty-millimeter mortars"—which included Charles Kelly.

As they drew closer to Altavilla, the platoon came upon an Italian man. Second Platoon was fortunate to have *three* Italian-speaking GIs within their ranks—Gatto, Survilo, and La Bue—all of whom intently listened to the local man. "The Italian didn't seem to know where the Germans were," said Kelly, "or whether they were in the town or not, but we took what he had to tell us with a cupful of salt." Italy had formally surrendered the day before the invasion, "but we had been told not to believe it, for our officers didn't want us to feel relaxed and spoil the fighting edge we had worked up."

Still, Altavilla seemed to be friendly, and devoid of any Axis sympathizers. "They were all out shaking hands with us, and telling us they came from St. Louis or Brooklyn or other towns and cities all over the United States. They kept saying, 'I speaka Engleesh,' and bringing out bottles of wine and glasses. But we didn't have much time for that; we were busy trying to find places to set up our weapons." The company commander then ordered Kelly to carry the unit's water and ammunition stores into the mayor's house—"a big, solidly-built, very beautiful building," Kelly remembered. "But first, he wanted me to be sure that the house was free of Germans. We checked every room on the first floor, leaving a man in each room. Then I went up the stairs, and found a girl ducked down under some blankets on a bed"—presumably the mayor's daughter. "I pulled the blankets back and motioned for her to get out," to which she complied, but not without yelling and cursing up a storm. Understandably, the young girl was irate at the sight of American GIs taking over her family's home. "Still yelling, she went downstairs to join her family. Men began hauling ammunition in through the door and setting up machine guns in the courtyard and in the windows. Before it grew dark, we had changed that building into a fortress-arsenal."

During the night, however, the Germans occupied a nearby hill, one-half mile away. Their position on that hill gave them an excellent redoubt over the American positions in Altavilla. The town itself was on the slope of a hill which, as Kelly recalled, featured a road at its base, leading ten miles out to the beach. "The mayor's house fronted on the town square, and both were in the uphill half of the town," said Kelly, "near its outskirts and overlooking the road." This meant that the Germans atop the nearby hill would have a clear line of fire to the mayor's house and the American outposts. During the ensuing battle, Kelly recalled that the Germans came down their hill, "and also down the slopes of the hill upon which the town was located."

The next morning, just as Kelly was preparing to eat breakfast, the German machine gun nests opened fire. "They had a beautiful field of fire," he said, "and knocked out one of our machine guns in the courtyard." Enemy bullets ripped into the GI machine gunners, and Kelly was aghast as he remembered that "the gun itself was sticky with blood, and had small nicks where the bullets had bitten into its metal. The men who had manned it lay around dead."

And, at this point, Kelly didn't even have a weapon. He had lent his rifle to a lieutenant the day before. "I had picked up two or three since then," he said, "but now I didn't have a gun. I felt naked without it." With enemy gunfire erupting all around him, he bolted upstairs looking for any available firearm.

As luck would have it, he found a BAR lying on the floor.

"I also found a pair of field glasses and, kneeling at a window, I could see men walking on Hill 315. The fire directed at us was coming from that hill, so I knew the men on it must still be Germans. I loaded my gun, waited a second to make sure my aim was true, and fired. When I picked up the field glasses again and took a look, three of the men who had been moving before were lying still. A fourth, who had fallen into a foxhole, was still moving one foot, so I upped with the BAR and let it chatter once more. When I peered through the glasses, that foot slowly straightened out and lay flat on the ground."

During a brief lull in the battle, a fellow GI (a lone machine gunner), plunked himself down at a window next to Kelly's, ready to lay down additional fire. "We spotted Gerry machine guns in the distance," Kelly continued. "Every time I'd duck down to load my BAR, the Gerry machine gun went into action. When I popped up ready to squirt lead, Gerry was busy loading."

The friendly machine gunner in the next window, however, wasn't so lucky.

He was hit through the shoulder, and began crying for a medic. But this wounded gunner wasn't the only soldier in peril. From the other rooms in the house, several more GIs joined the chorus of "Medic!" as they too were being hit by the incoming fire. Surprisingly, one of the first "medics" on the scene was a German POW who had been a doctor before the war. The GIs wrangled him over to the wounded, ordering him to render medical aid. "That Kraut doc really knew his trade," said Kelly. "In no time at all, he was fixing up two of our wounded for every one [that] our own medic was repairing."

By this time, Kelly had fired his BAR so much that it literally ceased to function. "When I put the next magazine load of cartridges in it, it wouldn't work anymore."

Kelly was dumbfounded, but he had no time to troubleshoot the weapon.

He had to keep returning fire.

"I laid it against a bed, went into another room to get another BAR, and when I got back, the bed was on fire. That first gun was so hot that it touched the bed off like tinder." Unfazed by the sudden inferno, Kelly took aim and began firing his new BAR until its barrel lit up with the reddish-orange glow of an overheated weapon.[1] With the barrel now warped from the excess heat, Kelly discarded the BAR, and began searching for another.

No luck. But he did find a fully-loaded Thompson submachine gun.

"So, I went upstairs…went to the window and gunned for some more Germans. There was no assurance that we would ever get away from that house. Any of us. We seemed a hell of a small island in an ocean

---

Kelly or one of his comrades must have extinguished the bed fire at some point during the battle. Or the bed may have been small enough to burn itself out, sans igniting the entire house.

of Germans. Yet I don't think any of us thought much about it. Not then, anyhow." To make matters worse, the Germans were descending into the town, and the battle was devolving into a close-quarters street fight.

By now, Kelly had burned out two Browning Automatic Rifles, and was using all the ammunition he could find for his Thompson submachine gun. When his Tommy gun ran dry, he picked up the next available weapon he could find—a bazooka. "Now, I picked up a bazooka," he said, "and crawled among our dead men in the upper floor, looking for bazooka shells. Those shells weighed about four pounds each. I brought down six of them, and put one in…but it wouldn't go off. I worked on that bazooka for a while, then poked it out of the window and pulled the trigger. The men in the house thought an 88-mm shell had hit the place. All the pressure came out of the back end of that tin pipe, along with a lot of red flame, and the house trembled and shook."

Kelly fired that bazooka four times before he spied a box of dynamite on the floor. He asked his platoon sergeant if they could use it, but to no avail—"we had no caps or fuses." Lying beside the dynamite, however, was a small incendiary device. "I threw that at the roof of a nearby building the Germans were holding," he said. "It exploded there and the house started to burn." Capitalizing on that momentum, Kelly picked up a 60mm mortar shell, pulled out the safety pin, and tapped it on the window ledge, making it a live round—"or, the way I planned to use it, a live bomb." For if the mortar shell landed on its nose, it would provide the necessary percussion weight to detonate on impact. As Kelly looked out the window, he could see a handful of Germans coming up a small ravine by the rear of the house. "I whirled that shell around and let it drop among them. I did the same thing with another shell. As each of them landed, there was a cracking roar, and when I looked out again, five of the Germans were dead."

With no mortar rounds left, Kelly went searching for yet another weapon. Grimly, he found his third BAR in the hands of a dead comrade on the third floor of the house. "His ammunition was lying in the belt beside him," he recalled, "but he didn't have much of it left." Thus, Kelly found some machine gun cartridges of the same caliber, and put them into the BAR magazines. "Then, I took it down to the front room and started to squeeze its trigger. Another man, three or four feet away, had an M1 rifle. Every once in a while, he got excited and stood up to shoot. But he tried it once too often. Peering from my window, I could see a stream of tracers coming from off in the distance," one of which hit the rifleman next to Kelly, passing right through his shoulder. "He slumped down to the floor, blood poured from his shoulder," followed by the inevitable cries for a medic.

Kelly, meanwhile, continued to bullseye German soldiers with his *third* BAR of the day. "Snipers were touching up the men down in the kitchen," he said, "and someone sent for me to go down and help." When Kelly got there, however, he was aghast to see his fellow GIs *cooking spaghetti*, nonchalantly as if nothing else was happening. They were gingerly going about their kitchen routines, "just as if they were chefs in a ravioli joint back home and food was all they had to think about." Kelly continued: "They had spread tablecloths, had laid out knives and forks, had sliced bread, watermelon and honeydews, and had put out grapes and tomatoes."

Kelly was beside himself.

Here they were, in the middle of a life-and-death firefight, and these GIs were setting up meals as if it were a five-star restaurant. They didn't even seem to care that the German snipers were drilling holes into the kitchen windows. "I don't mind people doing screwy things," he said, "it helps to let off steam sometimes when things are so tight that otherwise you'd go off your rocker, but to see them readying that meal made me mad."

Kelly blew up at his comrades, but his remarks didn't faze them.

"Ah, quit blowing your top, Kelly," they said as they continued stirring their spaghetti. "So, I thought, the hell with it. Maybe they've got a good idea there."

With a shrug, Kelly found the nearest box of champagne, broke the neck off a bottle, and took a hearty gulp. "Then I took the straw off a big basket, got out three or four eggs, broke them into an empty C ration can and drank them raw. Still tasting those eggs, I went over to the window through which those snipers' bullets had been coming. Nobody had been paying much attention to the snipers; they had been having their own way and had grown careless about concealment. I saw one of them in a tree, and drew a bead on him. His rifle dropped from the tree first; then, after a few seconds, he toppled down limply to the ground himself. While I was squatting there, one of the men from upstairs came down with about fifty BAR magazines, lay beside me and began feeding me ammo. On a distant hill, tanks were firing at us. I took a look at them through a pair of field glasses, and saw a Heinie on top of a turret, shooting at us with a 20mm cannon. I fired about twenty magazine loads at him."

After firing the first 15 magazines in rapid succession, this gun's barrel, too, was turning red. But Kelly fired the remaining five clips for good measure. Looking through his field glasses once more, he could see that the turret was down, and one of the Panzers had fled the scene. Deciding to give his red-hot glowing BAR a rest, Kelly took a swig of champagne—the first he'd ever had. "To me, it tasted like soda pop, and after drinking it I felt full of gas bubbles." Back at the window, he spotted a lone German soldier coming towards the house by way of a small gully. By now, the BAR had cooled off, and the barrel had returned to its normal graphite hue. But when Kelly pulled the trigger, the BAR wouldn't fire.

"I pulled it again, but it still wouldn't fire."

Even when he threw a bullet into the firing chamber, the BAR couldn't produce enough pressure to ignite the propellant, "so I had to let that German come ahead," he said wryly. "He was coming from where our troops were supposed to be, and it dawned on us that the Germans had separated Company K from Companies I and L, and built a circle around them. We were running low on ammo and we had almost given up hope of relief. Our only communication with the world outside the mayor's house was our radio, and the Germans had jammed that. They had gotten hold of one of our radios, tuned to the same frequency we were using, and all we could hear over our set were Germans talking."

Miraculously, the house-bound GIs found a hand-set phone radio, and re-established contact with 3d Battalion Headquarters. After a few minutes of back-and-forth radio chatter, Battalion agreed to let the GIs in the mayoral home withdraw after nightfall, escaping under the cover of darkness. "In the meantime," however, "we were to stay there and fight."

As daylight faded, Kelly and his comrades gathered up the remaining ammunition and started a decoy firing pattern on one side of the house while the GIs escaped out from the other side, six men at a time. "There were about thirty of us left alive," Kelly remembered. "The lieutenant broke us down into groups of six men each, and at intervals those groups drifted away." Those who remained behind kept firing to cover the retreat. "I offered to stay as part of the rear guard," said Kelly, "and Bill Swayze, a six-foot-five GI from Trenton, New Jersey, said, 'I'm going to stay, too.'" Kelly remembered Bill as a "fast talker" with a perennially cheerful disposition. Even in the heat of combat, "he had grinned all through the battle," said Kelly, "and he was good company."

After the last group of GIs had exfiltrated the house, Kelly crawled out with Bill Swayze, the lieutenant, and another GI from K Company. "We took with us the wounded who could travel. The ones who were hit too badly to move we left there. We heard Germans coming into the house behind us. Then I heard guns going off upstairs. Our guns. The wounded had saved a few rounds for a last fight. The Germans yelled 'Surrender!' but the firing didn't stop short; it gradually flickered out."

Stealthily sneaking their way out of town, Kelly and his friends came upon their unit's communication wire. "It was like finding a street you know after wandering around lost in a big city," he said. All they had to do was follow the landline…and they'd eventually find the unit's command post. "Miles farther along, we heard somebody yell the word, 'Hollywood!'" said Kelly—the challenge to which they would have to provide the password. The so-called "challenge" and "password" was a long-standing tradition in the Anglophone armies. It was a security measure to verify any unknown persons lurking beyond a unit's perimeter. A sentry would yell the challenge word—in this case, "Hollywood"—to which the other soldier, if he were in the same unit, would know the password reply. "Luckily, I remembered the answer to that challenge," said Kelly, "and called back, 'Theater!'" As a general rule, passwords were carefully selected based on phonetics that the enemy would have difficulty pronouncing. For example, Germans typically pronounced "th" as if it were a "z." This gave rise to using passwords like "Theater" and "Thunder." For if a password were compromised, and a German tried to use it in hopes of gaining entry into an American position, the GIs could spot the imposter by hearing him say "*Zeater*" or "*Zunder*." The same logic held true in the Pacific, where passwords were deliberately chosen by the letter "L" (i.e. lollipop) because the Japanese pronounced the letter "L" as an "R."

"Sixteen of our men had been waiting with their rifles on us, ready to let us have it, if we'd given the wrong countersign," Kelly continued. Among them were several of the men who had escaped from the mayor's house in the earlier groups of six. After taking a quick head count, the lieutenant in charge gathered up the survivors and ran towards the nearest confirmed Allied position.

But for his actions on September 13, 1943, Charles Kelly was awarded the Congressional Medal of Honor. It was the first Medal of Honor awarded to a soldier in the European Theater. After receiving his medal, Kelly returned stateside, where he toured the US as part of the Army Ground Forces "Here's Your Infantry" demonstration team. It was, by all accounts, a PR "Dog-and-Pony Show"—selling war bonds and demonstrating various battle techniques. When the tour ended, he was assigned to the Infantry School at Fort Benning, Georgia. He received his Honorable Discharge in the summer of 1945 at the rank of Technical

Sergeant.

Years later, Kelly reflected on his actions at Altavilla. "I've had people ask me what a man thinks of at a time like that." Most people expected him to say that a soldier thinks of home, or wonders if his soul is ready to meet the Almighty. "The truth is," said Kelly, "once a man is in action, he thinks very little about home or the hereafter…and most of his thoughts are focused on finishing the job at hand."

As Kelly recalled: "A GI has to work out his own philosophy of fighting." Early on, Kelly adopted a mindset of continuous positive affirmation. In other words, he *refused* to die. "If I ever let myself go into battle thinking, 'This is one battle I'm not going to come out of,' I'd be no good as a soldier, and I probably wouldn't come out of it. Once in a while, anybody gets scared. But if you don't think about it, it doesn't last. One of the things that helps drive away fear is actually seeing, the enemy. It's patrol work and fear of the unknown that gets on your nerves. Then, too, having a buddy killed snaps men out of the jitters."

Unfortunately, Kelly's return to civilian life was marked by personal tragedy. In 1946, he opened a service station in his hometown of Pittsburgh. However, he was forced to sell it the following year after a robbery and a downturn in business. That same year, his first wife Mae was diagnosed with cancer, which ultimately took her life in 1951. The cost of her radiation treatments eventually drove the Kellys into foreclosure, and they lost their home. After Mae's death, Kelly's sister said: "He went out of control after that and was never the same again."

Having lost his wife and his business, Kelly took a series of odd jobs—working as a security guard, house painter, and construction worker—none of which he held for very long. However, a reprieve of sorts came in 1952, when General Dwight D. Eisenhower ran for president. The former Supreme Allied Commander asked Kelly to help him on the campaign trail. While at a campaign stop in Louisville, Kentucky, Kelly met Ms. Betty Gaskins.

They were married six weeks later.

Still, he couldn't ignore the harsh realities of civilian life. He was running out of money, and was being rejected by every potential employer he sought. In a 1952 interview, Kelly admitted: "When you're in combat, you have a job to do; you know how to do it; and you know you can do it. But these years have been rough. Your hands are tied. You have a thing to do, but you can't do it. You go in and ask a man for a job. It's a job you never had before, and you're asking for it. And you get so many 'No's.'"

However, the story of Kelly's plight as a hard-luck war hero became a media sensation. Newspapers throughout the country ran stories about him, drawing attention to the fact that a Medal of Honor recipient should never have this much trouble finding gainful employment. Money donations poured into the family, along with more than 100 job offers. Kelly purportedly accepted a job with a scrap iron company in St Louis, whose owner provided financial assistance for Kelly to purchase an eight-bedroom home. However, Kelly quit the job before his family even had a chance to move in.

But soon thereafter, Kelly seemed to have gotten another lifeline. Kentucky Governor (and former Senator), AB "Happy" Chandler, arranged a job for Kelly as an inspector in the State Highway Department. It was a steady job, and one that paid $340 a month ($3,514.35 in 2022 money). Still, by the time of his appearance on *The Mike Wallace Interview*, Kelly's wife Betty said: "Chuck deserves a better deal from his country; he did something special as a soldier, and now he should get some kind of special consideration."

But things only got worse for Charles "Commando" Kelly. He kept his position in the State Highway Department until April 1961, when he called Betty to say that he was going to Cuba to fight Fidel Castro. He ended the call with a promise to set up a trust fund for her and the kids, but instructed her not to try to find him.

Charles Kelly never returned home.

For the next 15 years, Betty had no idea of his whereabouts. In 1962, she divorced him in absentia, and raised their children as a single mother. During his self-imposed exile, Kelly began to drink more heavily, and became an itinerant worker, moving from Kentucky to California to Texas, and finally re-settling on the East Coast. Sometime in the 1970s, Kelly was involved in an auto accident in Washington, DC, whereafter he was hospitalized for nearly a year with a fractured skull and broken legs.

In 1984, Kelly resurfaced at the VA Hospital in Pittsburgh. After several decades of hard drinking, his kidneys and liver were failing. He had taken the bus to the hospital and told the VA clerk that he had no living relatives, even though his children and five of his brothers were still alive. On January 11, 1985, Charles Kelly facilitated his own death by deliberately pulling the treatment tubes from his body.

He was 64 years old.

He was buried at Highwood Cemetery in Pittsburgh. To this day, no one knows the whereabouts of his medals.

14
THE LONGEST WINTER

CHARLIE HAUG:
A REPLACEMENT IN THE "BLOODY BUCKET" DIVISION

A native of Sleepy Eye, Minnesota, Charles "Charlie" Haug enlisted in the Army on February 19, 1943. He completed Basic Training at Camp Wolter, Texas; and was initially assigned to the 92nd Infantry Division at Fort Leonard Wood, Missouri, before leaving overseas as a "replacement." Being a replacement was inevitable for many soldiers during times of conscription. As the name implied, their job was to *replace* an individual soldier who'd been killed in action. However, that fallen soldier often had strong ties to the comrades he'd left behind. Thus, the "replacement" was often seen as an outsider—someone who had to prove his worth, and try to make friends among the battle-hardened veterans in his company. Very often, replacements came and went so quickly (i.e., killed or wounded) that their platoon mates avoided getting to know them. Charlie Haug expected as much when he departed the US aboard a troop carrier on September 12th, 1944.

In fact, every GI on that ship was a designated "replacement," not knowing where he'd ultimately be assigned. They only knew that they were headed to Europe. "Each man had just been issued new clothes and a new rifle, and all 4,000 on the ship were being sent as replacements in units that had been shot up during the Allied advance across northern Europe to the gates of Germany." By September 1944, Italy was firmly in Allied hands, and the invasion of France had been rolling back the tide of Nazi aggression. In fact, it seemed that the Allies would be in the Fatherland by Christmas. But little did they know that certain pockets of the *Wehrmacht* were about to catch their second wind, and launch a counteroffensive in the Ardennes Forest.

Haug's group landed at Omaha Beach near the end of September. Although it had been three months since the Normandy invasion, the beach still bore the unmistakable scars of combat. "In either direction," he said, "all we could see were wrecked ships and landing barges." The torrential rain that greeted them as they arrived on Omaha Beach only added to the somberness. And, as they stepped onto the steep cliff leading from the shore, Charlie caught his first glimpse of the American cemetery. "As we looked at these thousands of crosses, we realized for the first time just how many men can be killed in a single battle." Each one of these graves marked the body of a man who had fallen on D-Day.

Following a series of marches, truck rides, and a five-day journey inside a cramped "Forty & Eight" boxcar, Charlie arrived at the frontlines near the German-Belgian border on Veterans Day—November 11, 1944. His final destination was Company B, 112th Regiment, 28th Infantry Division. Known as the "Keystone Division," the 28th was Pennsylvania's federalized National Guard unit. More recently, they had earned the nickname "Bloody Bucket," owing to their bright red, semi-trapezoidal unit patch. The 28th Division was among the hardest-hit units during the bloody, brutal fighting in the Hurtgen Forest. The battle had cost them more than 6,000 casualties, hence the need for replacements like Charlie.

When he reached the survivors of Company B, however, it was a "pitiful sight." As Charlie remembered: "They had been in the attack for eight constant days, and there was only a handful of them left. Their clothes were all caked with mud, their faces were all dirt and grease. None of them would say a word to us. They just sat there and stared. Occasionally, one would drop his head between his knees and sob like a baby. They had had enough. They didn't want us to replace their buddies whom they had just seen fall, because this meant that they would have to go up into it again. They immediately made each of these poor men a sergeant, and they put them in charge of us green replacements."

The reluctant sergeants made Charlie a "platoon runner"—a messenger between his platoon and the company command post. The 28th Division then moved north into Luxembourg, relieving a unit that had been on the line for nearly a month. By this time, the weather was getting colder, and the first snowfalls had begun. Still, Charlie didn't find life on the frontlines all that bad, minus the occasional artillery attack. Company B was, after all, facing a portion of the Siegfried Line, and the Germans were hunkered down inside a network of well-constructed pillboxes.

Charlie shared his foxhole with two other "runners," but the three of them made their earthen abode livable with a layer of straw; and they burned bark inside an old oil drum for warmth. Throughout the night,

Charlie Haug.

each of them stood guard in two-hour shifts. Their twice-daily meals were served only during the hours of darkness (9:00PM and 4:00AM), so the enemy couldn't see them walking around. "As December began, the extreme cold forced the company to move into the small German town of Lutzkampen," which was much closer to the *Wehrmacht's* main line of resistance. The Division's outpost in Lutzkampen was fairly secure— "except for one day when a German patrol wandered into town and killed a GI who was souvenir hunting." Charlie then had the unenviable task of hauling his dead comrade back to the rear. While carrying the body of his deceased friend, Charlie's pants were soaked by the blood. And it would be two months before Charlie could get another pair.

Being from Minnesota, the cold weather didn't bother Charlie much, but trench foot was a persistent problem in the ranks. Some men found that when they removed their boots, they were unable to put them back on because their feet had swollen so badly. "The troops were issued new socks and overshoes that were two sizes too big." After a few weeks, however, the collective swelling went down, and the men returned to wearing their normal sizes.

There was very little action in Company B's sector until the pre-dawn hours of December 16, 1944. The previous night, December 15, Charlie had stood guard from 10:00PM until Midnight, and got four hours of sleep before rotating back onto his guard shift. "Little did I know," he said, "I had just had my last real sleep for the next ten days."

Suddenly, at 5:10AM, the sky erupted with the sights and sounds of German flares. "The whole sky had become light, just like dawn was breaking and it was two hours early. What the hell happened? Who turned on the light switch? It took about a minute before we finally got out mouths closed again." The artillery battery supporting Company B responded, firing multiple volleys into the suspected German positions, but with little success. Shortly after 6:00AM, the Germans initiated their own counter-battery fire, punctuated by an infantry advance on Lutzkampen. Two American outpost were quickly overrun as the sounds of German gunfire filled the air. "This was our initiation into the famous Battle of the Bulge," said Charlie. "We didn't realize it yet, but we had been caught directly in the middle of a German attack."

The gunfire waned at around 7:00 AM as the Germans consolidated their forces around Lutzkampen. By 7:30, however, they renewed the attack. "Out of the still darkness came the awfullest screaming and yelling you would ever want to hear. The Germans were coming. They were screaming, and they were less than 100 yards in front of us. How they got so close without our hearing them, we'll never know. There was a steady stream of lead pouring from their guns. Many of their bullets were tracers, and the red streaks snapped in every direction."

Still, the GIs had the upper hand.

They were concealed by their foxholes, and the Germans were exposed, offering clear and silhouetted targets. "During the first half hour of the battle, our men had some pretty easy pickings." But Company B had suffered some serious casualties as well. Their company commander was killed in action, as were the two medics who tried to save him.

By 10:00 AM, the Germans' hasty counterattack had failed. Those who had survived began waving their white handkerchiefs. As Charlie began wrangling the first of these German POWs, he was surprised to see that many of them were just young boys. "The oldest was perhaps about 18 and the youngest about 14." Moreover, these young conscripts began to pelt the GIs with numerous questions, like: "Will I be sent to New York City?" These German boys seemed anxious to see America.

In this opening firefight, the Germans had lost 135 men. Company B had held their ground, but their sister companies on either flank had been cut down. This left the 90 surviving men of Company B to spread out over a defensive front nearly one mile long. "We still had some faith left in the American Army though, and we prayed that other outfits in the rear would be able to stop the Germans and push back up to us. We had lost contact with our division, but we didn't have any orders to withdraw, so we had to sit tight."

By 3:00 PM on December 16, the main body of the German attack force reconsolidated at Lutzkampen. Company B hunkered down, but they no longer had "priority of fires" for artillery support. To make matters worse, all of their machine gunners had been killed. Later that evening, the Germans renewed their assault, this time with half a dozen Panzers in the lead. The first Panzer came within 50 feet of the outpost American foxhole; but this was no garden-variety German tank—it was a *Flammpanzer 38*, a flame-throwing combat vehicle. And it wasted no time unleashing its fiery death onto the first two GIs in its path. "The two kids sat there helplessly as a gigantic stream of roaring fire shot in on them. Their worries were over. All of us on the hillside [Company B's current position] saw this, and we knew we were next. It terrified our guys, and many of them jumped up from their holes and ran back over the hill into the thick woods behind."

Charlie and a few others stood their ground, but to what possible avail?

They had no anti-tank weapons in the foxholes, and certainly nothing that would stop a *flamethrower* tank. But as the lead Panzer got within 200 yards of Charlie's foxhole...a miracle happened. From another hillside nearly a quarter-mile away, an anti-tank gun from a sister unit began to fire on the incoming Panzers. "The first few shells missed, but suddenly the lead tank burst into flames. Soon, the second and third tanks were hit, and a few seconds later the fourth and fifth tanks were burning." The final Panzer beat a hasty retreat.

Saved by the anonymous angel gunner, Charlie sprang to his feet, going from foxhole to foxhole to count the living and the dead.

His numbers were heartbreaking. Of the 90 men in Company B, only 18 had survived.

And the one remaining lieutenant (who was now the company commander by default) told his men to keep standing strong. As night fell, the young lieutenant surmised that a quick artillery strike might eliminate the German ground troops in Lutzkampen.

It was a solid idea. But at this point, could the artillery even support it?

Given the high volume of fire missions, the howitzer batteries had likely run out of ammunition. Still, it was worth asking. But with all their communications down, the GIs' only method of inquiry was to send a runner…a job that inevitably befell Charlie. "Ken Jenne [a fellow trooper] and I were ordered to contact the artillery," he said. Normally, Ken and Charlie would have no issue sending the request. But today, their anticipated path to the artillery unit would take them through enemy-held territory…in broad daylight.

Not surprisingly, Ken and Charlie had walked barely 200 yards before the Germans opened fire. "They started firing mortar shells on the hillside we were climbing," said Charlie. "About 15 shells landed around us, but we were not hit by shrapnel."

It was the second miracle Charlie had experienced that morning.

A few moments later, Ken and Charlie came upon the Forward Observers' outpost…but all he found were their discarded rifles, helmets, and cartridge belts. "The men had evidently been captured just hours before"—thus robbing the howitzer batteries of their essential spotters. Dismayed but not discouraged, the two runners headed farther west to find the gun batteries. But as they made their way across an open field, they were quickly greeted by a hail of grazing gunfire, and the unmistakable roar of a Panzer's engine. Neither Ken nor Charlie attempted to gauge the direction of the gunfire; *they just started running.* "The machine gun bullets were kicking up snow…and the shells from the tank's gun were ripping up the treetops." With so many friendly and enemy units intertwined along the Ardennes front, it was often hard to gauge who was firing at whom. But given the intensity of the fire, and the telltale sound of German equipment, there was little question as to who was firing. Years later, at a Battle of the Bulge reunion, Charlie recalled that: "Jenne told the group that normally when a person runs, their legs go one in front of the other. But as we crossed the field that day, he said mine were going all the way around."

After what seemed like an eternity, Ken and Charlie reached the thick of the woods, out of sight and range from the German ground fire. A few hours later, they ambled into the fire base of the 229th Field Artillery. Surprisingly, at the fire base, Charlie found several of his comrades from Company B who had fled from the previous day's Panzer attack. The bad news, however, was that the artillery battalion had, in fact, run out of ammunition. Ken and Charlie briefly considered walking back to Lutzkampen, but decided it would be a "suicide mission." Instead, the remnants of Company B, along with the 229th Artillery, headed farther west at nightfall.

The ragtag GIs travelled through the open country until they came to a road, which they followed for nearly a mile. The road led to a bridge, guarded by two German sentries at its entrance. The GIs killed the guards and crossed over the bridge, but the presence of these two guards was a telltale sign that there were other Germans nearby. Thus, the Americans dispersed into the woods, heading west at their own pace.

A few hours later, they came upon an abandoned town where other American stragglers had congregated. "We now had a few men from every company in the 112th Regiment, and they all told the same story," Charlie recalled. "They had been attacked on December 16, and most of their men had been killed or captured." Still, these battered Americans decided to form a defensive perimeter around the town. Charlie was put in charge of running ammunition to the outpost machine gun teams. Later that same day, however, the Germans advanced on the town. Charlie made only *one* round trip to the machine gun team before it was overrun by enemy Panzers. Realizing it had become a "no win" situation, Charlie and the other GIs made a break for the forest.

They escaped farther west, keeping a steady pace until the afternoon of December 18. By now, they were fighting off exhaustion and the much-maligned adrenaline dump. "As we lay there, we realized for the first time that we were mighty hungry. Some of our guys had not had a bite to eat for three days now." Some of the retreating soldiers had scavenged food from the town they had just departed; and Colonel Gus Nelson (the ranking officer in the group) ordered the remaining food to be divvied up among the men. "Each of us got a little something to chew on," said Charlie.

As the group hunkered down for the night, they were unexpectedly joined by five other GIs from Company B. As it turned out, these five wayward soldiers were all that remained of the sixteen men whom Ken and Charlie had left behind at Lutzkampen. Now, this hodgepodge of GIs from the 112th Infantry and 229th Artillery huddled together, trying to conserve body heat. "It began to snow during the night, and it was still snowing when dawn broke on the 19th of December." Under the cover of this snowfall, Charlie and his comrades moved out along the first road they came upon. The following day, they came upon another American unit where they dug in and repelled a series of German attacks throughout the 20th and 21st.

The battered GIs were holding their own, but the bigger question was: "Where was the rest of the Army?" These isolated pockets of soldiers seemed to be all alone in the Ardennes, fighting off whatever German probes came their way. "There seemed to be no help coming from anywhere," said Charlie. "We ourselves had now retreated about 30 miles since the first day of the attack, and it looked like the only thing we could do was retreat again." More to the point, their morale was falling. Two of Charlie's comrades had shot themselves in the foot, hoping to earn a ticket home. Instead, the two men were left behind with their self-inflicted wounds as the rest of the group retreated farther into the woods. "Everybody was hungry and tired and cold. Whenever two or three of us got together, we would always find ourselves talking about whether or not we should give ourselves up the next time we were attacked." There was no sign of help; and every day the Germans seemed to be gaining more strength. "We thought the Germans were winning the war."

With few options left, the officers of the group decided to leave a dozen troops at every major crossroad to slow down the Germans' advance, and perhaps buy more time for the main body of retreating American forces. As they came to the third crossroad, Charlie was among the next dozen selected to stand guard. "We were scared, and as we watched the rest of the guys head down the road, we were wishing we could be going with them. Soon they were out of sight, and we were left to our fate.

Two hours later, an American M3 halftrack zoomed by—but this halftrack was carrying German troops. It was another piece of captured Allied equipment. During the drive to the German borderlands, both sides had captured and impressed vehicles from the other. And this formerly American halftrack was followed by a long convoy of enemy trucks.

Charlie and his friends, realizing they were outnumbered and outgunned, beat a hasty retreat into the woods. Part of the German contingent caught up to them near a village on the other side of the woods, whereupon two of Charlie's friends were felled by machine gun fire. Charlie himself was running so hard that he lost his helmet as he dashed into another thicket of trees. "We must have run for an hour steady," he said, "and then we were so exhausted we all stopped, threw ourselves on the ground and rested. Our lungs ached."

By now it was dark, and the men suddenly realized it was Christmas Eve. "We didn't have the slightest idea where we were," he said, but they decided to continue west. Soon they came upon a river, which they estimated to be nearly 100 yards wide. Not keen to making a river crossing in the dead of winter, the men looked for a bypass…until they heard the incoming mortar attack. The shelling, however, was American. Indeed, the rounds were passing over their heads, and landing in the opposite direction. Charlie and his friends then realized that they were getting closer to friendly lines, and thus waded across the river.

A short time later, the ten GIs came upon a Belgian farmhouse, whose occupants gave them bread, but warned them that several thousand German troops were in the area. Once back on the road, Charlie met the first other Americans he had seen in days. As luck would have it, a small convoy of Jeeps came around the bend, picking up Charlie and his battered friends.

But their luck ran out nearly as soon as they had found it.

For within only a few moments, the convoy was intercepted by a German patrol. Two of Charlie's friends, Frankie Jordano and Warren Quimby, were riding in the lead vehicle and were taken prisoner. However, when the Germans noticed that Warren was missing a leg from a prior battlefield injury, they decided to kill him rather than tend to his wounds. "They saw Quimby's leg was gone, and a German pointed a rifle at Quimby's head." Panicking, Quimby raised his arms and shouted "No! No!" but it was no use—"there was a loud crack and Quimby's body bounced back on the ground. He felt no more pain."

Charlie himself was a bit luckier. His Jeep was farther down the line, far enough to give his driver time to throw it in reverse. But as the Jeep crested a nearby hill, the driver met an enemy bullet. Charlie and a few others fled into the woods, but two of their number were wounded during the escape. One comrade caught a bullet to the neck, but was still alive; the other caught a bullet to his gluteus muscles. The latter could walk, but he could no longer sit down. Another man in the group, Lieutenant

Mayer Goldstein, one of the few surviving officers, was nursing earlier wounds in both of his legs.

"Our three wounded guys were exhausted," he said. "The kid that was shot in the neck kept falling down all the time, and was getting awfully weak from the loss of blood. We knew that we couldn't keep going like this much longer, so we decided to head for town. If the Krauts were in town, we'd give ourselves up."

Given the circumstances, it seemed like their only option.

"No matter which way we went, we ran into Germans," said Charlie. "The woods were full of small groups of Americans trying to survive." Because Charlie was the only man in the group who still had a rifle, the senior sergeant ordered him to go into town and make the overtures for surrender.

Racked by hunger pangs and lack of sleep, Charlie stumbled towards the nearest house in the village. As he got nearer to the house, an angry voice rang out from the darkness.

"Halt!"

Charlie threw down his weapon and raised his arms, signaling his surrender.

But that same angry voice then cried out: "Who the hell are you?"

Charlie had just surrendered to a paratrooper from the 82d Airborne Division. Indeed, Charlie and his battered friends had accidentally wandered into the 82d's area of operations. Nearly 1,000 paratroopers had occupied the town, making their final preparations for an eastward counterattack. "Three of the wounded were transported to an aid station, and the other five were debriefed on where they had seen the German concentrations." Charlie and his friends were then sped to the rear, where each of them ate the "biggest meal you'd ever want to lay your eyes on. We really ate."

Charlie spent the next few weeks recovering from his ordeal while more replacements flooded into the 28th Division—"filling up the depleted ranks." On January 5, 1945, the reconstituted 112th Infantry Regiment (now manned mostly by replacements), was sent back to the frontlines, ready for an attack on the German-held town of Spineux, Belgium. The Americans quickly gained the upper hand, and the Germans began to fall back. "It was the first time some of us had ever seen the Germans back up, and it did us a lot of good," said Charlie.

Unfortunately, many of the new replacements were "trigger happy" (i.e., nervous and having trouble adjusting to the newfound stress of combat). As a result, "several GIs were killed by their own comrades." Still, the enemy was on the run. The following day, after a 12-minute artillery barrage, Charlie's unit took Spineux. "The fighting was house to house, but by nightfall, the town was held by the battalion and 200 German prisoners had been taken."

And it would be the last hurrah in the ETO for Charlie Haug.

"This was the last combat action we saw in the Bulge," he continued. "Our 28th Division was now ordered to a rest area in France."

As the Allied campaign dragged on, Charlie's unit was then ordered south to attack the German-held city of Colmar, a city on the River Rhine, just north of the Franco-Swiss border. Charlie would have participated in the attack, but the torturous winter of 1944–45 had taken a toll on his feet. Indeed, by March 1, a debilitating infection had rendered him unable to walk. It was the consequence of his feet being frozen, thawed, and re-frozen several times throughout the campaign. While convalescing at an Allied hospital in Paris, however, Charlie heard the news of V-E Day. The Nazis had quit; and Charlie's unit had now been designated part of the "Army of Occupation." He rejoined the remnants of Company B, serving this time as the company clerk until the unit returned stateside in July 1945.

After the war, Charlie returned to his hometown of Sleepy Eye, Minnesota, taking a job at First Security Bank of Sleepy Eye. Two years later, on August 4, 1947, he married the former June Enebo in a small ceremony at the Lake Hanska Lutheran Church. Charlie and June made their home in Sleepy Eye, where they ultimately raised five children. Charlie, meanwhile, continued working in the finance industry. In 1968, he became President of the First Security Bank, a position he held until his retirement in 1990. But even in retirement, he spent the next several years preparing Income Tax Returns for the bank's depositors. Charlie Haug passed away on May 4, 2017 at the age of 94.

15

GI JACK OF ALL TRADES

Tom Stafford: From Quartermaster, to Combat Engineer, to Rifleman, to Career Officer

Tom Stafford was the eldest of two children born to a small-town agricultural family. Born in rural Virginia in 1923, Tom came of age during the Great Depression. And, like many families in his community, he had grown accustomed to *both* parents working to support the family. Said Tom of his mother: "She was a housewife until the Depression hit and then she went to work. My dad, he owned and operated four farms"—three of which were contiguous to each other. "The other farm, the fourth one, was about a mile up the road." Each farm yielded a variety of crops and livestock—including hogs, cattle, chickens, tobacco, and corn. Still, even during the worst of economic times, the Staffords fared better than most. "As far as the Depression was concerned, we always had plenty of food and as I remember our clothing was always good; and my dad was able to hold on to all the farms."

Like many of the Greatest Generation, the New Deal was a defining aspect of their lives. The so-called "Alphabet Soup" of New Deal programs (including the CCC, TVA, and WPA) sought to put Americans back to work and improve their quality of life. At times, however, it seemed like many of the New Deal programs were "make-work" projects. "I remember one time sitting out on the front porch of our house…looking across the street, and there were a group of men cutting the grass," he recalled. "There were nine people and they had two lawnmowers. And they were cutting the grass with those two lawnmowers." Finally, a neighbor went up to the man who appeared to be in charge and said: "I want to know why you need nine people to cut the grass when you only got two lawnmowers." The man replied: "Well, ma'am, this is a WPA project; and we have to have two to come and two to go, two to sit, and two to mow."

"Well, that's only eight," she replied. "What's the ninth person do?"

"That's me," he said, "I'm the supervisor."

Tom graduated from high school in May 1941, with the goal of attending Virginia Tech. But even with a solvent family, tuition rates along with room-and-board would be a steep cost. Tom's dad said: "Well, you know it's a pretty expensive proposition," but he offered his son a deal. If Tom was willing to spend a year at home, working and saving enough money to cover the first year of college expenses, the elder Stafford would pay for the remaining three years. "So, I stayed out of school, went to work for Brown & Williamson [a prominent tobacco distributor], worked a year, saved all my money," and enrolled at Virginia Tech in September 1942.

The attack on Pearl Harbor the previous December, however, had modified his plans. "I remember hearing about it," he recalled, "and we went down to the Gulf Oil station and everyone was saying, 'Well we'll whip those Japs' ass inside of a week.' Damn fools." It seemed that no one was anticipating a four-year struggle in the Pacific that would end with the first nuclear weapons ever used in warfare. But, with war on the horizon, Tom joined Army ROTC and enrolled in the Corps of Cadets. Virginia Tech was among a half-dozen Senior Military Colleges, or "citizen-soldier" schools, who hosted a Corps of Cadets separate from the general student population. Each member of the Corps was required to participate in the ROTC program, and many took commissions as officers in the Armed Forces.

But his ROTC career was cut short when he was unexpectedly drafted in March 1943. The draft age had been 21 until mid-1942, when President Roosevelt lowered it to 18. Given his ROTC background, Tom was familiar with at least some of the military customs and courtesies. "When I got drafted it was in March of 1943, and I lived in Petersburg, Virginia. They shipped me down to Camp Lee [present-day Fort Lee]… it was a Quartermaster Center but they had a basic training center there." After completing his basic training, he applied for OCS, but "I was told I was too young to lead troops in the Quartermaster Corps." As somewhat of a consolation, however, the Camp Lee cadre offered to make him an NCO through the proverbial "shake-and-bake" Non-Commissioned Officers School—where in as little as 90 days, a high-performing soldier could earn the stripes of a technical sergeant. "So, I went in and took that course and it turned out that the NCO course was almost identical to the basic OCS." Just another example of the Army's bureaucratic inefficiency.

From Camp Miles Standish outside of Boston, Tom boarded the HMS *Empress of Australia* (an old British cruise ship turned troop carrier), and set sail for England in November 1943. "We landed in Liverpool," he said, "and then from there I went down to Birmingham," to the Replacement Depot in Lichfield where he awaited orders to a gaining unit. As luck would have it, Tom arrived at perhaps the *worst* Replacement Depot in the Allied footprint. "This place became infamous," he said, "and, in fact, the commander was later court-martialed for the horrible conditions [within his camp]. His name was Killian; and they called it Colonel Killian's Concentration Camp." Killian was a notoriously toxic leader, and many a GI dreaded spending any amount of time within his Replacement Center.

Normally, incoming GIs like Tom were supposed to stay 4-5 days at the depot before getting their follow-on orders. But after a week had gone by with no orders, Tom took matters into his own hands. He and his friend, Mel Sadler, went down to the Replacement Center bulletin boards, looking for any announcements of units seeking volunteers. "We saw this notice on the board for volunteers for a particular unit. It didn't say what kind of unit; but, hell, we'd have done anything to get out of there. So, we put our names in, and we were told to load up everything in our duffle bags and be ready to move out early that evening." Tom and Mel then climbed aboard the two-and-a-half-ton troop carrier truck, eagerly anticipating their new unit…and equally anticipating a reprieve from Colonel Killian's toxic command climate.

"It seemed like we drove all night long but…when they finally stopped and it was daylight, and when they opened that tarp [the covering on the back of the truck] and I looked out, I thought I was in Florida—palm trees, tropical foliage, and everything else. We wound up in Torquay, England, down in Devonshire…the southern tip of England; and we found out later that the reason that all this tropical vegetation existed was because the Gulf Stream came up the east coast of America and went across the North Atlantic. That warm water helped the tropical vegetation grow." Stepping off into the seemingly out-of-place tropical landscape, Tom and his buddy learned that they had volunteered for the 6th Combat Engineer Amphibious Special Assault Brigade.

"It was a top-secret outfit," said Tom. And three such brigades had been assigned to the European Theater. Of course, as a trained Quartermaster, Tom knew *nothing* about being a Combat Engineer. But he was certain that he could learn anything with the right amount of on-the-job training. All incoming members were assigned to live in British homes. "There was no barracks, no mess hall, no nothing," Tom remembered. "Everyone lived in private homes, two of us to a home." Tom and his buddy Mel were assigned to live with a greengrocer. "This guy owned a little grocery shop that specialized in vegetables and canned goods."

Seven days a week, Tom and his fellow GIs would assemble at different locations throughout the English countryside, learning the fundamentals of combat engineering—demolitions, obstacle emplacements, and hasty fortifications. Typically, every GI got the evening to himself, and was free to do what he pleased, so long as he remained within a certain mileage of his home billet. Tom and his friends used it as an opportunity to mingle with the British residents. He soon discovered, however, that the English language seemed to be the only thing they had in common with the British.

One evening, for example, Tom attended a local dance catering to American GIs and British Tommies. After the dance was over, the band played the *Star-Spangled Banner*, to which the GIs stood at ramrod attention. Then, the band broke into a chorus of *God Save the King*. At first, no one took offense; but the American GIs heard the tune and mistook it for *My Country 'Tis of Thee*, unaware that *God Save the King* had the same melody. Thus, when the GIs started singing *My Country 'Tis of Thee*, it started a fight between the Americans and the indignant British troops. "We didn't know the difference," Tom admitted, "but we soon found out."

Diplomatic gaffes and cultural ignorance aside, the GIs spent many a week training alongside their Allied partners for the upcoming invasion of Europe. By the summer of 1944, most of Italy was in Allied hands, but to truly effect the conquest of Europe, the Allies would have to invade Northern and Southern France. By all accounts, Northern France had to be the priority. And Normandy was the focus of the Allied entry.

During the lead-up to the invasion, Tom and his fellow sappers conducted a number of rehearsals at Slapton Sands on the shores of Devonshire. Slapton Sands inadvertently became a flashpoint during the war because of the disastrous invasion rehearsals. During these dry-run invasions, several Allied troops were killed by friendly fire, and a handful of US naval vessels were sunk by German PT boats. In all, these poorly-executed invasion rehearsals cost the Allies more than 700 casualties before D-Day even started.

By the fifth of June, however, Tom felt that many of the growing pains, false starts, and hiccups had subsided. They were ready to invade Normandy. From their launch point in Weymouth, Tom's brigade had initially taken off on the night of June 4, among the designated "first wave" of troops to hit the beach. "We got half-way across," he said, but "the channel was so rough that they decided to turn around and come back." Realizing they had lost the element of surprise, the Allied Command decided to wait another day, launching late on June 5, with anticipated landfall on the morning of June 6, 1944.

"We were supposed to land on Omaha," said Tom, and at a draw called Les Moulins…and that was about 1,000-1,200 yards, from our first objective which was a little village called Saint Laurent-Sur-Mer." Tom and his platoon of sappers were expected to hit the beach shortly after H-Hour (6:30 AM). Like most troops going ashore, Tom's platoon was riding aboard a tactical landing craft, a British variant. "Wasn't very long as I recall, couldn't have been more than 100 feet. It was big enough to carry several deuce-and-a-half trucks, and some jeeps, couple of platoons of infantry and combat engineers." The landing craft itself was crewed by US Coast Guardsmen—"two sailors and an ensign," recalled Tom.

Because Tom and his fellow sappers were crouched behind the landing ramp, they couldn't see the gut-wrenching carnage of the Normandy landings.

But they could certainly hear it.

The bombs, bullets, and artillery shells, punctuated by blasts of water, were a stark reminder that they were headed into harm's way.

But just as the coxswain got ready to lower the ramp, he decided against it.

From his spot at the helm, the coxswain had a front row seat to the blood and carnage playing out on Normandy beach. And he didn't want his men to become a statistic before they even left the beachhead. As Tom recalled: "he wasn't going to lower that ramp because we'd have been slaughtered getting off." Instead, he winched the boat back into the shallows, and vectored farther down the beach, out of range from the heaviest machine gun fire. Thus, instead of getting off at Les Moulins, Tom's platoon landed farther down the beach near Vierville-Sur-Mer.

"I recall that we waded about 100 yards or so through the surf," said Tom, "and all I remember is making a mad scramble getting up to a sea wall," which in turn led to a paved road running parallel to the beach. As Tom got halfway across the road, however, he encountered his first friendly casualty. "I saw a body lying there," he said, "an American face-down, and decided to pull him over to the side of the road." Grabbing the fallen comrade by his shoulder straps, Tom dragged him to the edge of the road, but when he turned him over: "Lord, half of the guy's face was shot off." Tom noticed, briefly, that this dead GI was a Ranger captain. "That surprised me," he said, "because the Rangers were supposed to land at Pointe Du Hoc. I couldn't figure out why there would be Rangers there." Years later, Tom discovered that the fallen captain was part of a Ranger company that had somehow gotten separated from the rest of the Ranger Battalion.

Scrambling to the top of a nearby hill, Tom looked back to the beaches of Normandy, now several yards below. "I'll tell you, it was just mayhem and bedlam. German artillery was coming in and mortars, etc., and I remember seeing one lone American 105 howitzer that had been able to get ashore. There were a lot of amphibious tanks that were supposed to get ashore but very few of them made it. This one howitzer, boy, I thought it was an automatic cannon. These guys were firing, it looked like they were firing 10-15 rounds a minute"—an impossible feat for even the most experienced cannon crew. Years later, Tom discovered that the furious 105mm howitzer was, coincidentally, one of two guns commanded by his cousin, Brad Stafford, an artillery officer in the 29th Division. He survived the war, too," said Tom, "but he's long since passed on."

Also coincidentally, Tom's unit was tasked to support the 29th Division, helping them get across the beach and supporting them as they moved farther inland. "I remember a couple of days after we got ashore, a British commando, believe it or not, showed up." He had been separated from his unit at one of the other beaches, "I guess on Gold or Juno Beach," Tom added. "He joined up with us and stayed with us for several days."

After the breakout from Normandy, Tom's career as a GI took an interesting detour. As a reward, of sorts, for having survived the D-Day invasion, Tom was inexplicably reassigned to a POW stockade, guarding German prisoners. But after three weeks of babysitting indignant Nazis, "I got fed up with that," he said, "and I went in and told them I wanted to go back to a regular unit, either back to my old unit [the special engineer brigade] or some other unit, but I didn't want any more of that POW guard business." The stockade commander granted Tom's wish, but told him that he would likely end up in a regular infantry division.

"That's OK by me," Tom replied.

Thus, Tom Stafford was thrown back into the replacement network, and by December 1944 he was a new rifleman assigned to the 87th Infantry Division. "I don't know exactly where we were at the time" he said, "but I recall landing in Luxembourg City to join the 87th, and found out that the Bulge had just broken out. We were told we're going to hold you here [at the replacement depot] in Luxembourg City in case the

Germans break through and attack." And that's where Tom stayed until early January. The rest of the 87th Division, meanwhile, had been pulled from Metz and attached to the Third Army for the relief of Bastogne.

Finally, in January 1945, Tom joined the 347th Infantry Regiment, "and I was assigned to L Company…2d Platoon." From there, Tom spent the remaining winter months manning a number of frozen outposts along the western battlefront. They went from Bastogne to Bonnerue, then back into Luxembourg along the Sauer River, then to St. Vith, and finally Belgium, where they managed to drive the *Wehrmacht* back into Germany. "Things were rough," he recalled. "When I got to 2d Platoon, I don't think there were more than 20-25 men in the platoon. Normally, the strength of a platoon is 41 men, one officer and 40 enlisted men." Yet, throughout his tour in the 87th Division, he never saw the platoon's end-strength exceed more than 30 men.

Like many of the units that had been thrown into the Battle of the Bulge, Tom's platoon was manned almost entirely by replacements. Most of the original non-commissioned officers in the company had been killed or wounded. And among the replacements, "none of them had had any prior combat experience." The new non-commissioned officers were enthusiastic but, as Tom said: "They just didn't know how to lead. I found that out in a hurry. We had a fairly good lieutenant but he didn't last too long." Indeed, the lieutenant was killed in action and, to make matters worse, the platoon sergeant sustained a critical wound, which led to his evacuation. This left Tom Stafford as the senior-ranking sergeant in the platoon. "And so, the company commander, Captain Kidd, told me to take over the platoon as acting platoon leader." As a young sergeant with less than two years of service, Tom Stafford, the young quartermaster-turned-sapper-turned-rifleman was now an acting platoon leader. "I remained acting platoon leader until the end of the war," he said bluntly. "Got a battlefield commission right there at the end."

By the end of March 1945, Tom's unit had broken through the Siegfried Line and crossed the Rhine River at Koenigstuhl. They had expected the river crossing to pass without incident, but Tom's unit met fierce resistance on the opposite side of the Rhine. At a nearby town called Braubach, Tom instantly recognized the source of his troubles: "There was a big castle on the other side of the river overlooking Braubach," he said. "We were told, at the time, not to fire on the castle because it was one of the few castles that hadn't been destroyed in all the wars the French and Germans fought. The castle was called Marksburg Castle." Despite its protected status as a historical landmark, the Germans had been using it as an artillery observation post. "They had complete command of the river," said Tom—for miles in either direction.

Tom's platoon was barely halfway across the river when the Germans opened fire. "They were dug in right there on the banks of the river," he said. "They had dug trenches and covered them over with turf and bushes and there were machine gun nests in there and they had…this observation from the top. They had put 20mm anti-aircraft guns on the hills overlooking the town, and they had depressed those things and they were firing those at us." His platoon fared well, losing none of its men during the river crossing—"but a couple of the other platoons didn't fare as well," he added. "We lost one of our best platoon sergeants. At this time, all four platoons in L Company, with the exception of one, were being led by the platoon sergeants."

L Company succeeded in taking Braubach, while their neighboring K Company stormed the Marksburg Castle. Tom, in the meantime, captured two Germans in Braubach who were overlooking the Marksburg Castle redoubt. After a brief interrogation, one of the captured Germans revealed the location of their commo line, which Tom's platoon hastily cut, thereby severing all communication between the castle-bound forward observers and the artillery guns along the hills.

"Then from Braubach," he continued, "we moved to a little town called Bad Ems, then from Bad Ems I captured a German general." It appeared to be a stroke of good luck; for it wasn't every day that an American GI captured a Nazi general. Moreover, this general was dressed in civilian attire; and, at first, he gave no indication that he was a high-ranking officer in the *Wehrmacht*. The clandestine general might have avoided detection, but as the GIs were searching his home, Tom found the general's uniform.

"He admitted that it was his," said Tom. "I think he was home on leave or something."

But whatever the reasons for his out-of-uniform appearance, Tom made the general put on the uniform and marched him back up the road to the L Company commander.

Not far ahead, Tom had another surprise encounter.

"We found a POW camp," he said, "had a bunch of American prisoners, British prisoners," the most senior of which was a British Sergeant Major.

After liberating the multi-national POW camp, Tom recalled that "we began to move pretty fast, going across Germany." In fact, he called it somewhat of a "merry chase." For by now, the *Wehrmacht* was in full panic as the Americans were closing in from the west, and the Soviets from the east. "We got on the autobahns,"—the legendary superhighways that indirectly inspired the US Interstate System—"and that was one of the very few times I can remember loading up in trucks, or on tanks, and riding. Finally got to a place, Zella-Mehlis, I remember. Then we began to run into resistance at a place called Saalfeld. Lots of resistance there." Indeed, from Saalfeld, the Germans were blowing up every bridge behind them, doing whatever they could to slow the Allied advance.

By now, it was April 1945, and "most of the units we encountered were *Wehrmacht*, which was the German regular army, and sometimes we'd run into SS." But on other occasions, they ran into the *Volkssturm*. Literally translated as "People's Storm," the *Volkssturm* was a national militia levied by the Nazis during the latter months of World War II. "Most of them were old men," said Tom, "and when I say old, most of the guys had fought in World War I. The rest of them were 14- and 15-year-old boys. We called them 'Hitler's secret weapon.' They were 14- and 15-year-olds armed with *panzerfausts*...the German version of the bazooka."

From Saalfeld, Tom's battalion led the regimental attack on Plauen. "My Company L was given the mission of leading the way into Plauen," he said. "We got halfway into Plauen and Captain Kidd [the company commander] got a message from an artillery spotter plane." These observers had just spotted a platoon of Germans preparing to demolish the one remaining bridge over the Elster River—the tributary running through the heart of Plauen. "As Captain Kidd got the message that the Germans were setting demolitions under the bridge," Tom continued, "he called me on the radio and told me to move my platoon through... and to see if I couldn't keep the Germans from blowing up the bridge."

To affect the capture of Plauen, a section of tanks (two Shermans) had been attached to L Company, providing direct fire support to the infantry. "Kidd gave me the two tanks," said Tom, "and I put a couple of squads right in front of the tanks." As they made their way to the site of the suspected demolition, however, they were surprised to see very little resistance. "We were really surprised," Tom added, "because this town had a lot of factories and ordnance plants"—one of which was manufacturing tanks. To boot, there were several warehouses where the German Army had purportedly cached weapons and equipment. "We figured the Germans certainly would put up a fight to try to keep us from capturing that," Tom explained, "because that stuff was sorely needed by them."

But this piecemeal resistance had grown to a deafening crescendo by the time they reached the river. Seeing the Germans on the bridge, Tom directed both tanks to open fire on the German dismounts, "to try to scare them," as he said—"scatter them so we could get across the bridge and keep them from blowing it." The German sappers, realizing they were outgunned and overmatched, beat a hasty retreat across the river, leaving their detonation assets where they lay. "I cut the wires that were leading down to the demolitions they had placed under the bridge." Tom discovered later that, by preserving the bridge, he had saved a historically-significant piece of engineering. "That old bridge had been built 250 years before Columbus discovered America," he said. "It was the oldest stone-arch bridge north of Italy."

Having saved the bridge, captured the fleeting Germans, and secured the city of Plauen, L Company then moved into the town of Theuma, near the Czech border. At around this time, Tom had his first look at the Buchenwald concentration camp. Buchenwald was nearly 30 miles from their current location, and had been liberated by the Allies only a few days earlier. "General Eisenhower wanted every division that was close enough to Buchenwald to go there," said Tom, and see just how horribly its inmates had been treated.

At first, Tom didn't know what to expect.

Was this "Buchenwald" just another POW camp?

When Tom came through the front gates, however, his jawed dropped. "I tell you, that was one horrible, horrible sight…bodies stacked up, dead bodies…everything you read about, all the pictures you see of Buchenwald, they were absolutely correct. The bodies stacked up, and I remember also…seeing a bunch of German civilians from the town of Weimar ordered into the camp to take a look at what the Nazis had done."

Tom quickly realized that this was no POW camp.

But he couldn't immediately deduce the camp's purpose. At first glance, the prisoners seemed to have nothing in common. There were Jews, Poles, Gypsies, Slavs, political dissidents, and handicapped persons. Moreover, there was nothing in their background that should have warranted their imprisonment. Tom soon discovered, however, that the Nazi regime had imprisoned them for being "undesirables," and liabilities to the Aryan race.

By mid–April, Tom's regiment had been ordered into a holding position. "We were told to hold up, not to move it any further, wait for the Russians." Indeed, on the Eastern Front, the Soviet war machine had been beating back the tide of Nazism. From Moscow to Stalingrad, the Red Army had reclaimed its territory lost during the early days of Operation Barbarossa. Through Ukraine, Belarus, and Poland, Soviet forces had overrun the *Wehrmacht* and were striking into the heart of Germany.

"Finally, we got the word right after the first of May to move out again," said Tom, "and so L Company's objective was a town called Jaegersgrun," which they occupied with relative ease. As they secured the town, L Company was elated to hear the news of Adolf Hitler's suicide, followed soon thereafter by the news of V-E Day.

But although the war in Europe had officially ended, L Company had no time to celebrate. "We had our hands full taking care of all these German prisoners," said Tom. At one point, however, Captain Kidd gave Tom permission to take a truck across the border into Czechoslovakia and find any brewery willing to sell beer in exchange for German *Reichsmarks*. Luckily, Tom didn't have to go far to find an obliging brewmaster. "We went into Czechoslovakia," he said, and got three or four kegs of beer"— all in exchange for a wad of German *Reichsmarks*.

On May 12, 1945, Tom wrote the following letter to his father in Virginia:

"Dear Dad,

Just a few lines to say hello and to let you know I'm well and OK and hope that you're fine and feeling all right these days, too. I've been planning to write for the last few days but honest, Dad, we're really keeping on the go.

Since I wrote you last, lots has happened, hasn't it?

Yes, what I've been praying for a long time finally made up its futile mind to happen. Now when you shoot a Kraut, they call it murder, which all goes to show just how nonsensical war really is. Just by signing a little piece of paper a man can change the life and destiny of millions, and those who yesterday had the sole purpose of killing his fellow man can now laugh, joke, smoke and give food and shelter to those same people.

Well, it's beyond me.

I suppose the American Army and the rest of the Allies have become so powerful that they can afford to forget some of their original purposes...

Dad, this may be a little hard to believe, but your son had two complete German infantry divisions surrender to him, as well as a number of other assorted enemy organizations. I'd always wanted to see what the enemy really looked like; so the day before the peace was signed, my jeep driver and I took off, and we wound up at a general staff meeting where one Lieutenant General surrendered his division and then we went on through the lines where another General surrendered also.

Dad, I've always thought of your advice, and as far as that's concerned, the war hasn't changed me one bit. So, without further fanfare, I come to you for some more of it. I don't know whether I mentioned it or not, but I've been put in for a battlefield commission. That's well and good, but I also understand that officers don't count in the point system. As an enlisted man, I probably stand a good chance of staying away from the CBI [China-Burma-India Theater] and prospects for a discharge. If you were in my shoes, what would you do? I've just about made up my mind, but I'll wait to hear from you; what you think? So, write soon.

Lots of love,
Tommy."

Tom Stafford ultimately accepted that battlefield commission, although the process of receiving one was rather morbid. To earn a battlefield commission, the existing lieutenant had to have been killed in action, or permanently evacuated from the battlefield. Taking command of the platoon (or what remained of it), the next-senior sergeant would become the acting platoon leader and, if his performance warranted it, he was recommended for a commission.

"The recommendation would have to be endorsed by the battalion commander, and the regimental commander…then it would go on up to the division commander, and that's where the final decision was made. I think the division commander had been given authority by the War Department to promote people to commissioned rank. I had my bars pinned on by General [John] McKee who was the assistant division commander." Ironically, McKee was a graduate of the Virginia Military Institute (VMI), which had a long-standing rivalry with Virginia Tech. And McKee, well-aware that he was pinning bars on a former Virginia Tech student, said with a chuckle: "I never thought I'd see the day when I'd be giving anybody from [Virginia Tech] anything."

Accepting the commission allowed Tom to stay with his unit longer. By now, he had already amassed enough "points" to earn his ticket home. The points system (officially, the "Adjusted Service Rating Score") determined when a GI could earn his eligibility for an early discharge. "You needed at least 85 points," Tom recalled. "You got points for the number of months you'd been on active duty. You got points for the number of days you'd been in combat." A GI could also earn points through various decorations like the Bronze Star, Silver Star, etc.

But accepting his commission took him out of the points system, and he never regretted it. "I wanted to stay with my men." Typically, however, if a soldier earned a battlefield commission, they would transfer him to another regiment. "They certainly wouldn't allow you to stay in the same company or even in the same battalion."

But Tom refused to leave the men with whom he had shed blood.

In fact, Tom had made it a non-negotiable condition of his acceptance. He told his chain of command: "Hell, I'm not going to leave these guys, and if I can't stay with them as a commissioned officer after having led them for four months in combat, then keep the damned commission." Surprisingly, the regiment yielded to his demands.

But although the fighting in Europe had ended, the Pacific War raged on. "We were the first division pulled out of Europe in order to make the invasion of Honshu," said Tom. "In fact," he continued, "we were brought back to the States in July and we were given a 30-day leave…then we went down to Fort Benning…to be re-outfitted and get replacements and get re-equipped." They were about to be loaded on a train westbound to California, then depart San Francisco for the anticipated invasion of Japan.

Fortunately, the war ended before Tom could steam out of San Francisco Bay. After his division was deactivated in October 1945, Tom Stafford decided to stay in the military. In his first postwar assignment, he was selected to be the Aide-de-camp to General Phillip Gallagher, Commanding General of the 25th Infantry Combat Team at Fort Benning.

The following year, Tom accompanied General Gallagher to Occupied Germany, again as his Aide-de-camp when the latter became Deputy Commanding General of the US Constabulary. This assignment gave Tom a front-row seat to the burgeoning "Cold War"—a war to be fought not necessarily with bombs and bullets, but with words and ideas. The "hot" battles would be fought mostly by proxy, and at the farthest corners of the earth. Words like "Mutual Assured Destruction;" "Nuclear Holocaust;" and "Balance of Power" would steer American foreign policy for the next forty-plus years.

When Tom Stafford returned to Germany as part of the US Constabulary, he saw the harsh realities of the post-war Reich. Many within the Nazi High Command were put on trial at Nuremberg for their part in the Holocaust. Understandably, most Germans were still shocked and embittered by their defeat at the hands of the Allies. To make matters worse, their country had been partitioned along ideological lines. East Germany was now a Communist state and West Germany was a fragile, ailing democracy. The economies of both nations were in shambles, millions were starving, millions more were homeless, and several had taken to a life of crime.

Upon his promotion to Captain in 1950, Tom was awarded command of a rifle company in the 1st Infantry Division, whose regular mission was to secure the German–Czechoslovakian border. In 1953, he began his first tour in Korea, taking command of a Headquarters Company in the 7th Infantry Division. The following year, he became the Civil Affairs Officer for the 25th Infantry Division, and oversaw the division's redeployment to Hawaii. Tom stayed with the 25th until his next tour in Korea, from 1960–61, as the Budget Officer for the Eighth Army. His final assignment was in the Office of the Comptroller, Military District of Washington, where he served until 1963. Having completed twenty years of active service, Tom Stafford retired at the rank of Major.

But even in retirement, he continued to serve the Department of Defense, working as a civilian comptroller until his final retirement in 1987. At this writing, Tom Stafford and his wife, Gayla, are living quietly in Fairfax, Virginia.

16

BLOOD ALLEY

PETER WIRTH (USMC)
AND THE BATTLE OF OKINAWA

It was the last losing battle for the Imperial Japanese Army. But it was a long, grueling fight for the soldiers and Marines who pummeled the island into submission. On June 5, 1945, Company L (3d Battalion, 5th Marines) was in a tight spot. They were pinned down under heavy fire from *two* Japanese machine gun nests. As the casualties began to mount, the situation seemed hopeless. Company L could not advance, and they had nowhere to hide. But one of the young Marines, PFC Peter Wirth, suddenly decided that he had had enough.

"I could sit there and die, or I could go out and do something about it."

Without orders, he grabbed his rifle and charged the machine gun nests. His actions freed the company from its peril and earned him the Navy Cross.

Peter Wirth was another child of the Great Depression. Born on December 6, 1926 in the suburbs of Chicago, Pete spent most of his formative years in Iowa. Amidst the economic hardships of the era, he quit school after the 8th Grade. Not one for being idle, however, he joined the National Youth Administration (NYA)—one of the various New Deal agencies that aimed to mobilize America's young work force. Through the NYA, Pete trained as a machinist, landing jobs with International Harvester and the Rock Island Arsenal.

When he turned 17, however, he decided to join the war effort.

"I knew I'd be drafted eventually," he said. "I probably knew a few people who had joined the Marines, but to be honest, I didn't know one branch of service from another." At the age of 17, however, he was still a minor, and needed a parent's permission to enlist. His mother, perhaps reluctantly, signed his consent form; and in January 1944, he departed

Iowa for Camp Pendleton, California.

As expected, boot camp was an unpleasant experience. "I didn't care much for that," he said, "but it didn't last long." After graduation, the Marines offered him a 10-day furlough, but he turned it down. He had briefly considered going home to Iowa for his ten days; but he soon realized that the travel time would eat up most of his furlough. "It didn't seem worth it. I remember I had a grand total of $10 in my pocket, and I gave it to a buddy so he could go home."

Soon, Pete boarded a troop carrier to the western Pacific. Their final destination was Guadalcanal, where the new Marines underwent training for jungle and amphibious operations. Shockingly, part of the training included an exercise to see how long the Marines could withstand dehydration. "Well," said Pete, "the fact is you can't go very long without water no matter how much training you've had. But I suppose they did that for discipline."

He also recalled doing several hikes on Guadalcanal. "One time, we had to cross a river that was in full flood stage. Trees were going down all over the place." The trick to getting across this river, however, was to have two Marines wrap their gear into two separate poncho halves, snapping them together. The two Marines would then swim across the river, pushing the semi-buoyant poncho raft in front of them as they swam along. "The idea was to avoid anything like a tree bumping into you." But crossing a river under these conditions was a perilous task. Several Marines perished that day while trying to cross the river, three of whom were in Pete's company. "They drowned. Plus, guys were panicking and leaving their gear behind. We lost hundreds of rifles that day. And then when we got to the other side, they gave us some C-rations, and then marched us back to camp over a bridge that was just down the river. I'll never know for sure how many died that day. You don't get a lot of information out of the military."

The training on Guadalcanal was severe; but so was the situation that lay ahead. His next stop was Okinawa.

As the island-hopping campaign drew closer to the Japanese mainland, the Allies narrowed their gaze onto Okinawa. Located some 340 miles south of the mainland archipelago, Okinawa was the ideal location for an Allied airfield and staging area for the anticipated invasion of Japan. For their part, the Japanese High Command had also recognized the salience of the island, and committed 117,000 troops to its defense.

Peter Wirth as a young Marine in the Pacific.

Pete, meanwhile, had been assigned to the 5th Marine Regiment, and boarded another troop carrier en route to their new mission. At first, none of the onboard Marines knew where they were going. "Then Tokyo Rose came on the radio and told us…she said we were going to Formosa or Okinawa." The Marines couldn't figure out how this propaganda DJ got the information before they did; but based on their direction of travel, they knew she was likely correct.

But whether it was a lucky guess, or information delivered through the backdoor spy network, Tokyo Rose was correct that the Marines were headed to Okinawa. Along the way, however, Pete's unit made a daylong pit stop on a sandbar island, where the Marine Corps provided one last kegger before the invasion. "After a while," said Pete, "it got to be a problem. It was 110 degrees in the shade, and a lot of those people were not used to drinking beer. There were a lot of fights, but it didn't amount to much." But after they had all sobered up, the Marine expeditionary force returned to its ships, and stormed the beaches of Okinawa on April 1, 1945.

"I was up early, and they gave us the best breakfast I've had in the military. I don't know where they got fresh eggs out of the Pacific," he marveled. But the culinary euphoria was short-lived. For within moments, Pete flung himself over the side of the ship, descending down the rope ladder to the landing craft below.

"As soon as we got loaded, we barreled for the shore."

The undulating motion of the landing craft was made worse by the sudden onset of enemy mortars. Rounds began plummeting into the waves, splashing the innards of the landing craft with tepid seawater. "The guys driving the boats had their time just right," Pete continued. "The front end of the boat hit the beach, the front came down, and we took off out of the boat. The idea was to disperse as fast as possible so one mortar doesn't get you all. As soon as we were off the boat and lightened the load, he [the landing craft helmsman] was able to back up and go get more troops." Piloting the landing craft was a dangerous gig unto itself; the helmsmen often had to make multiple trips to deliver all the Marines to the shore. Naturally, this made them easier targets for the Japanese onshore batteries.

But aside from these mortar rounds, there was surprisingly little Japanese resistance on the beach. Operationally, the Army and Marine Corps had split the island in half, hoping to facilitate a "divide and conquer" of Okinawa. After a few days of reconsolidating, the Marines headed northeast, where they encountered only light resistance. Said Pete of these opening rounds: "I remember that we stalled around until we headed south to relieve the Army unit." In fact, the 1st Marine Division was conducting a relief-in-place with the US Army's 27th Infantry Division.

"I'm sure we had a lot more soldiers than the Japanese, but we hit tough resistance as soon as we went south. I think more Marines were killed and more ships went down in the battle for Okinawa than any

Pete Wirth poses with his uncle, who was also in military during World War II. Ironically, Pete's uncle was killed at the Battle of Okinawa, not far from where Pete's unit had made landfall."

other battle. At any time of night, you could look out and see Navy ships going down."

Seeing this action unfold before his eyes, Pete was admittedly nervous.

This was, after all, his first time in combat.

"I was kinda scared. But everybody else was in the same position." And it was not an easy position. "It was hilly, and very tough to go down...lots of fire, lots of casualties. It kind of came in spurts. I remember there was one hill near Naha [the prefectural capital of Okinawa] that we took twice, and got knocked off of it twice. The third time, we got to the top."

By June 2, the Marines had succeeded in pushing the Japanese to the southern end of the island, but not without heavy cost. It was on that day when Company L found itself under fire from two raging machine gun nests. With his fellow Marines dying all around him, Pete said: "It's hard to just stand there with people dying all around you. It's hard not to do anything. But we were pinned down. It was a quick decision. Either stay and die, or go out and die fighting."

He chose the latter.

Armed with his rifle, six grenades, and a .38 Special, the young Pete Wirth began his charge to the enemy positions. "I found that a short gun is handier when you're crawling on the ground. I had bought the .38 from somebody. Once you were over there, you carry anything you can get ahold of. Nobody cared." At first, another Marine accompanied Pete on his daring dash. But after a few yards, the comrade fell back under enemy fire. "It was probably about 200 yards I had to go," said Pete. "But of course, it felt like a couple or three miles to me."

As Pete came within striking distance of the first machine gun, he maneuvered to the side, out of the gun's traversing range. The Japanese had dug this machine gun nest into a cave; thus, the cave's walls provided Pete with all the flanking defilade he needed. "I pulled out a grenade, let the spoon go, and waited. If you throw it too fast, they'll just throw it back at you. You have to judge the time, but I'd thrown a lot in practice." Pete used up all his grenades to silence the first machine gun nest. But, in a stroke of derring-do, Pete sprinted back to L Company's position, running through the same gauntlet of fire from which he had come, and gathered *more* grenades to use on the second nest.

The second nest, however, would be more problematic than the first. It was higher up on the cliff, occupying another cave, thus making it harder to stay out of the machine gunner's sights. But with the help of some covering fire from L Company, Pete made it back up the hill to within sight of the second nest. At one point, he drew his pistol, and emptied it in the general direction of the enemy machine gunner.

"I didn't hit anything, but I didn't think I would."

Undeterred, Pete crawled up to the top of the cliff and shimmied his way over to the machine gun nest. Just as he had done with the previous nest, Pete ripped the pin from his hand grenade and tossed it into the cave's opening.

Thus ended the machine gun fire.

Climbing back down the cliff, however, Pete realized his work wasn't done. Back at the first nest, he discovered that two Japanese soldiers were still alive, which he quickly remedied with his M-1 Garand rifle.

Company L was now free to advance.

"At the time, you're too busy to be scared. When it's all over, the fear settles in. I was shaking a bit."

For his actions that day, Pete's commanding officer recommended him for the Navy Cross. In the Navy and Marine Corps, the Navy Cross was awarded for extraordinary heroism, second only to the Congressional Medal of Honor. Two weeks, later, however, Pete received an early exodus from the war, courtesy of a battlefield wound. "I was pursuing a couple of Japanese soldiers down by the beach. By this time, we were gathering up prisoners, but these guys didn't want to be prisoners, I guess. They went behind a boulder, and I didn't realize that one of them had doubled back and climbed on top of the boulder." The treacherous Japanese soldier shot Pete from above. The bullet struck his right shoulder, exiting through his back. The wound wasn't fatal, but it was enough to get Pete's attention. Yet, without missing a beat, the young Marine turned and killed his Japanese assailant. "I didn't feel any pain at all," he said. "It was just like someone hitting you in the shoulder. I never even dropped my rifle."

Still, his wound was enough to warrant a trip to the aid station. "There were bubbles in the blood coming out, so I knew it must have nicked my lung. Later on, it got to be more painful, and they shot me up with morphine, of course. There was a lot of pain as it was healing." Pete was then evacuated to a hospital in Guam, where he stayed until V-J Day.

Pete Wirth remained on active duty until 1946. For a time, he considered becoming a career Marine, but decided he had seen enough action for one lifetime. Ahead of his discharge, he traveled home aboard an aircraft carrier, where he recalled a funny story involving a sailor and his bicycle. This sailor, perhaps one of the deck handlers, was enjoying the postwar idyll by riding his bicycle along the perimeter of the flight deck. But whether he lost his balance, or was hit by a sudden gust of wind, this cyclist inadvertently rode his bike right over the edge of the carrier deck. "They fished him out—still holding the bicycle."

When he returned to Iowa, there were no bands, no ticker-tape parades, no homecoming events of any sort. His hometown newspaper ran a short story about his Navy Cross. But beyond that token acknowledgement, there was no fanfare for the returning war hero.

All told, it mattered little to him. Pete was proud to have served his country; moreover, he was happy to be alive.

After the war, Pete Wirth returned to his vocation as a machinist. He spent the next several years working for Mansfield Industries, tooling components for photographic equipment. He later worked for the Control Data Corporation; but when the company relocated, Pete negotiated to buy their tool and die machinery. With these new assets, he opened his own machine shop, running the business for nearly two decades before his retirement in 1988.

While building this career as a machinist and latter-day entrepreneur, Pete married Berthana Bergsrud in 1951, with whom he raised four children. Pete and Berthana were married for sixty-four years until his passing on December 3, 2015—just three days shy of his 89th birthday. He was proud of his service, but never attended any reunions. He likewise never wore his Navy Cross, and rarely spoke about his wartime experiences. But even in the twilight of his life, Pete never missed the opportunity to poke fun at his battlefield injury. His shoulder made a full recovery, but now and again, he could feel a tinge of pain where the bullet had dug its path. "When the weather changes, I can feel it," he joked. "I suppose there's some arthritis getting in there."

ABOUT THE AUTHOR

Mike Guardia is an internationally-recognized author and military historian. A veteran of the United States Army, he served six years on active duty as an Armor Officer. He is the author of the widely-acclaimed *Hal Moore: A Soldier Once…and Always,* the first-ever biography chronicling the life of LTG Harold G. Moore, whose battlefield leadership was popularized by the film *We Were Soldiers,* starring Mel Gibson.

He was named "Author of the Year" in 2021 by the Military Writers Society of America, and has been nominated twice for the Army Historical Foundation's Distinguished Book Award.

As a speaker, he has given presentations at the US Special Operations Command, the George HW Bush Presidential Library, the First Division Museum, and the US 7th Infantry Division Headquarters at Fort Lewis.

In 2022, he appeared in the History Channel series, *I Was There,* cast as a featured historian in the episodes on the Johnstown Flood of 1889, the Chernobyl Disaster, the Battle of Stalingrad, and the Oklahoma City Bombing. His other media appearances include guest spots on *National Public Radio (NPR); Frontlines of Freedom; Armada International;* and *Military Network Radio.*

His work has been reviewed in the *Washington Times, Military Review, Vietnam Magazine, DefenceWeb South Africa,* and *Soldier Magazine UK.* He holds a BA and MA in American History from the University of Houston; and an MA in Education from the University of St. Thomas. He currently lives in Minnesota.

Milton Keynes UK
Ingram Content Group UK Ltd.
UKHW021819041023
429907UK00006B/87